FIRST PLACE

Dog Writers Association of America

MAXWELL

2014

2014
FINALIST
New Mexico-Arizona
Book Awards

Our Most Treasured TAILS

Sixty Years of Pet Rescue

Kate J. Kuligowski

Proceeds from the sale of this book will be directed to:

Bro and Tracy Animal Welfare Inc.

Dixon Animal Protection Society

Fur and Feather Animal Assistance Inc.

Kindred Spirits Animal Sanctuary

All of these are New Mexico, volunteer-based,
501(c)(3), non-profit organizations.

This book is dedicated to my husband, Wally.
He has achieved the ultimate.
He has made our world a better one.

My husband, Wally, loves on Turner,
but love cannot conquer all.

ISBN: 978-0-615-8228-08

Library of Congress Control Number:
2013941554

THE GUYS™
PUBLISHING
COMPANY

905 Maverick Trail, SE
Albuquerque, New Mexico 87123

Photographs by Joyce Fay
and the albums of The Guys Publishing Co.

Edited by Richard McCord
Design and typesetting by Julie Melton, The Right Type,
www.therighttype.com

Printed in China
by Artful Dragon Press a U.S. Company

10 9 8 7 6 5 4 3 2 1

In memory of my grandfather,
my ChooDaddy, C.E. Smyer,
and my mother, Eileen Smyer Jacobson.

"Some of our greatest historical and artistic treasures we place in museums; others, we take for walks."

— **Roger Caras**

INTRODUCTION

These are actual events, about actual people and actual pets, most of which were rescues, from the pound, shelters, or the streets. Although the names of most of the individuals, places and pets have not been changed, it was important to change some of the names of our families, friends and neighbors, as well as of towns, businesses and organizations, to protect their privacy.

Bookstores and libraries have always shelved a number of real stories and books, heartfelt and well presented, about family pets. The very being of such a loving creature within a family necessitates many written accounts, which, like life, can be humorous, passionate and tragic. These stories are also reflective of the past and present lives of their owners, for it is their thoughts that define the telling of the stories. Hopefully the reading of these stories will continue to inspire each of us to become involved and make a difference in animal welfare in our communities and states.

This book shares with you our sense of enjoyment and fulfillment with these incredible 'throw-aways' and leaves you with many unanswered questions about why they became "throw-aways." Because it demands involvement from its reader, it is a valuable literary tool. It asks you to self-educate: to learn how animal humane legislation and education in your town, your county, and your state are handling this serious problem of animal abuse. It is the responsibility of all who respect life to ensure that the laws and practices involving the welfare of abandoned or relinquished dogs and cats reflect a humane society.

ACKNOWLEDGMENTS

Albuquerque, New Mexico— My husband and honey-heart, Wally, to whom I have been married for an incredible fifty years, is not only my greatest supporter but also that of the many pets we have rescued, fostered, and adopted. This book is as much his as mine. Without question, he accepted the care and responsibility of these abandoned pets, whose trust and affection he generously returned. While writing this book about those fantastic pets, there were times when I almost exhausted, simultaneously, his extensive vocabulary and his long-lasting patience. He is my hero.

Our son and computer whiz, Kurt, who helped me recognize and edit obvious storytelling flaws, has definitely earned my gratitude. He, too, for his whole life has loved and cared for these incredible dogs and cats. And, because of the special attention Kurt provided our bunch of rescues while Wally and I were on vacation, we could leave the house with an easy mind, which in its own right is priceless. Thanks to these two patient and special men whom I have been blessed to have in my life.

This book reflects the special skills of a friend and talented editor, Richard McCord, whose efforts made my book more readable, and thus more enjoyable, for you, my reader. He clarified my thoughts so that my stories would flow more smoothly, chapter to chapter. I am very thankful for his insight, guidance and professional abilities.

Julie Melton, because of her expertise and skills, was responsible for the final steps of readiness and polish before this book was sent to press. I am grateful to her for her timeliness and generosity and, most of all, for her many hours of donated time because of her strong belief in this book and its cause. Her talents created many innovative approaches in this books' presentation.

Any witty reference to nationally known individuals is strictly in good humor, with no disrespect intended.

Lisa and George Franzen have always been there for us, regardless, for over fifty years of friendship.

Joyce Fay of Bro and Tracy Animal Welfare Inc. championed our cause to save the badly injured Turner. The support that her organization and networking were able to provide to our Turner was ongoing. Joyce's professional talents were also responsible for several fantastic photographs, and her writing skills composed much of the sad chapter about Turner.

Over the years, many lost pets were reunited with their worried owners because the humane management of *Albuquerque Journal* and *Albuquerque Tribune* allowed free ads for lost and found pets. The *Journal's* weekly "Fetch" section is an excellent resource for humane education and welfare. Along with the City of Albuquerque, the *Journal* co-sponsors an annual "Fetchapalooza" adoption event. On behalf of New Mexico's pet owners, I salute their efforts.

Nancy Marano is the editor and board president of *Petroglyphs,* the award-winning resource publication for animal lovers in the greater Albuquerque area. She and her staff are diligent in assuring that pet owners be kept informed of pet-oriented gatherings, adoption events, pet services, and projects, as well as regional and national legislation (both current and pending).

A Corrales, NM, newspaper, *Bosque Beast,* fills its many pages with newsworthy articles affecting most animal-lovers in the Rio Grande locality. Its gifted writers and columnists contribute interesting and educational material about area wildlife as well as horses and domestic pets. I consider it a "must read" for all who appreciate and value animal life in our rural area.

Special recognition is due to the many kind and selfless individuals who have rescued or adopted rescue pets, as inconvenient, expensive, or even dangerous as it might have been. They, too, know that soul-lifting experience, that deep satisfaction of possibly saving and most assuredly changing the life of one of God's suffering creatures. My most heartfelt admiration goes to all who volunteer for animal humane organizations throughout America. These concerned individuals are the most effective weapons that our animals and children have in winning the fight against abuse and neglect.

TABLE OF CONTENTS

Wally, our son Kurt, and I shared a sunny afternoon with three of our rescues, Muffin, Whiskey and Buffy.

CHAPTER 1

A WIN-WIN SITUATION

"We give dogs time we can spare, space we can spare and love we can spare. And in return, dogs give us their all. It's the best deal man has ever made."

– M. Facklam

Wally, my husband, and I had always maintained that most rescue animals, pure-bred or not, make the best pets. That was because they had experienced the other side, the sad side, of pet care: neglect, abuse, and abandonment. Our family homes, for more than sixty years, provided the love, care, and shelter necessary to enrich and extend the lives of almost a hundred "thrown-away" pets, dogs and cats discarded in the streets or surrendered at shelters. Each one that we found and brought home has had entirely different issues than the others, but, with one exception, each was always accepted by the rest without overt posturing or incident, without turf growlings or markings. That was a remarkable feat for which we had no explanation.

Our family was always amazed by the genetic diversity among the canines we seemed to collect. [1]There are more than 350 breeds recognized by kennel clubs in the United States and abroad; the American Kennel Association recognizes 173 in its seven groups. Scientists have discovered that their wide assortment of body sizes and shapes, leg lengths, ear positionings, nose shapes, and fur colors, lengths and types, is due to fewer than fifty genetic switches. They explain that the reason for such a large number of different breeds can be attributed to the long history of dogs. They were first domesticated more than 15,000 years ago and since then have been bred for differing, chosen traits.

Our dogs ranged in size from Pugs, which we have had in our homes since 1964, to Great Danes. Pugs are often purchased because they are unbelievably cute and cuddly. But once the owner realized how heavily they shed, the health

---

1 Evan Ratliff "New Tricks From Old Dogs" *National Geographic,* vol. 221 no.2 (Feb,2012) pp 42-53

problems they incur with their bulging eyes and their loud, labored breathing, these cute pups can become street pups.

During all these years, our house had always been home to many adorable American Cocker Spaniels, probably discarded because of their tendencies to have difficult infections due to their wavy-haired long ears or because their pleading eyes can be subject to glaucoma in later life. Or maybe it was because of their propensity for barking, or just because they were an inconvenience. All of ours displayed a happy and obedient temperament.

Obviously, each breed, because of genetics, can be subject to different health issues and different behavioral traits. Irresponsible or uninformed owners use these as a crutch when explaining why they abandon or surrender their dog. Yet, this information is readily available on the Internet, an easy method to use when researching health questions, personality characteristics and possible quirks attributable to the different dog breeds. Those searching for a pet should be especially beware of the advertising by the unknowledgeable "backyard" breeders, whose puppies are a leading cause of shelter overpopulation due to health or temperament issues. It is prudent for the future pet owner to instead seek out legitimate, established breeders whose records reveal the health history of multiple generations, allowing them to screen for possible genetic problems such as hip dysplasia. This advice could save the new owner not only thousands of dollars in veterinary care but also the heartbreak of losing a beloved pet early in his life.

Presently Wally and I reside with total of nine terrific tails—two cats and seven dogs: a Pug, two Cocker Spaniels, a Cocker-cross, a Golden Retriever, a Labrador Retriever and a Chow Chow-Shar-Pei cross. We refer to them in mass as "the guys." Never has our permanent menagerie numbered greater than thirteen. When we have attempted to place a limit on the number we could care for, it became a dare for the Guardian of Homeless Pets. Within the month a stray would appear in our driveway, on our doorstep, or in our street. Their desperate and frightened appearance melted our hardened no-more-dogs defense system. We have even examined our curb, in vain, for the hobo markings (popular until World War II) designating our place as a "pet refuge," and the homeowners as "patsies."

Most of our rescues came with no collars, no tags, and no history. Most were of mixed ancestry, the most populous of all canines. Usually we hadn't a clue to the extent of the atrocities they had experienced in their past lives. Their visit to our veterinarian could only provide necessary medical care and a health profile. Only through the help of animal shelters and rescue groups with their devoted volunteers were we able to care for and usually place in well-matched homes, a multitude of discarded dogs and cats.

If our newly acquired rescue-dog was or could easily be socialized, showed no tendencies toward aggression, and was not impaired, he was usually adoptable. So we would foster him until a new and responsible owner was found. If his estimated age, a physical or mental disability, aggressive behavior, or the lack of socialization was cause for him not to be adopted, we worked patiently with him and ultimately made him one of "the guys," the number of permanent rescues that varies in our home, year to year. These are some of their stories.

It is understandable that most perspective pet owners shy away from the added responsibilities and financial burdens that are part of adopting a blind, deaf, medically-compromised, mentally challenged, or elderly pet. Wally and I remind ourselves, as we grow older, that someday those impediments might describe one of us. It is natural for all of us, not only the young, to feel impervious to aging and the ailments it slowly embraces.

Because unconditional love, regardless of age or infirmities, is the focus of Kindred Spirits Animal Sanctuary, we have tried to make the time to volunteer at this rural animal retreat in Santa Fe. In their peaceful and serene setting, eldercare and hospice is provided for dogs, horses, and poultry. Because most of our society holds the attitude that senior animals are disposable, Kindred Spirit sponsors tours, outreach programs, and workshops in hopes of changing that indifferent and calloused attitude. They teach that animals set the ultimate example of unconditional love, a philosophy from which our souls can profit.

We were among those readers of Joline Gutierrez Krueger's *Albuquerque Journal* column, December 2011, who were fortunate to be a part of one amazing outreach by Kindred Spirits, which was credited with an admirable and unusual rescue: five dogs along with their homeless mistress, who was hired to live and work at their facility, where her dogs could also be housed. That's definitely a double dose of Kindred Spirits' kindness.

We have rescued blind, deaf and aged animals. I observed a barrage of owner-surrender dogs and cats while working with Animal Humane Association of New Mexico and Watermelon Mountain Ranch Animal Rescue. Most of the owners relinquishing their pets seemed unashamed, without conscience, as they explained, "This dog is just too old."

There exists among the ignorant and indifferent a long-held concept that taking elderly or "bad" dogs and cats to the shelter or abandoning them is an acceptable practice. This is a cowardly, self-denial stance taken to absolve themselves from the guilt of being irresponsible, careless adults. "Bad" behavior can be the result of bad situations, bad expectations, bad training, mistreatment, misunderstanding, indifference and the absence of an individual's basic respect of life, to name but a few—a very few—causes of purported "bad" behavior for a pet (usually attributable to a "bad" owner).

The calloused pet owner who dumped his pet because "It is the pet's fault," completely misunderstood his responsibility as a pet owner, who is supposedly smarter than the pet. Accepted with ownership is not only the care but also the education of the pet. Laws dictate that the pet owner is to be held responsible for the behavior of that dog or cat. Fortunately, because of today's increased and enthusiastic ownership of pets, more states and communities have developed ordinances, statutes and laws to better define and monitor the responsibility of pet ownership.

This same train of thought could imply that children were placed in foster care because they were "bad." Although the life of a child can never be equated with that of a pet, they often share a common abuser. Too often child abuse follows prior abuse of animals, by the same deranged individual. Sixty-eight percent of battered women report spousal violence toward their household pets. Domestic abusers often kill, harm or threaten family pets in order to coerce family children into sexual abusive situations and to ensure that they remain silent about the abuse.

It should be a shared responsibility of all parents and all pet owners to be unceasing in their efforts to put a stop to this daily and unacceptable abuse and neglect of both children and pets by demanding a stronger level of legal and police protection for children and pets. After all, if you cannot respect all life, how can you respect yourself?

Irresponsible and unforgivable actions of parents and pet owners set the stage for my book's opening background chapters. They unveil the story of my first rescued dog, Sinbad, a lonely childhood, a complicated family history, and a childhood filled with tragic events. In those few formative years of my youth, it was the incredibly cruel and inhumane ("bad") behavior of a few adults that would shape my life's mission to seek respect for all living things. That determination would be evident throughout those eventful and exciting years we have shared with our assortment of adopted dogs. The joy they continually unleashed in our family was priceless. Our heartwarming experiences with our "thrown-away" pets have given us profound fulfillment and kindled the desire to continue.

I am finished with my tirade about people who abandon their pets. Congratulations if you lasted this far into this first chapter. Now let's get on with it and fast-forward to the "just plain fun" part of our pet ownership.

Although one pet is definitely an adventure, our lives with five to thirteen pets, at one time, constituted an entire amusement park with its roller-coaster rides, snack bars and, of course, barkers. We played the usual games in the grass, catch with tennis balls, tricks for treats, and rides in the car. "The guys" provided the reason for a number of long healthy walks, an excuse for patio parties, Pugnics or

Pugtober Fests. Without warning, they performed antics guaranteed to produce instant smiles and laughs. Those that were captured on film we used as greeting cards, framed and displayed. They were always shared with our long-suffering friends.

It would be an understatement that we thoroughly enjoyed our role as indulgent pet owners. Each pet has its own birthday celebration, Easter eggs, and personalized Christmas stocking filled with toys, and treats. An imprint of each dog's paw in concrete makes up our Parade of Pets on the patio. Thinking up humorous, yet affectionate nicknames for this crew was more fun than Scrabble. Wally, our son, Kurt, and I taxed our vocabularies, competing to find handles best-suited to their quirky personalities.

When any one of us was feeling disgusted, disappointed or down, my remedy for recovery was the company of a dog. One of the best parts of pet ownership was the fact that they returned our love, regardless. Our affection for them added new dimensions to our lives.

Although these activities keep us young, cheerful, and alert, one pet excursion definitely tugged on the limits of our pet-owners' patience. That dreaded trip was for their exams and inoculations at the veterinarian's office. Because of three-year rabies vaccinations, we were not forced to suffer this routine yearly. So it is only every third year that Wally, Kurt and I pack them in our Camry, front seat and back seat, usually four at a time, two trips minimum. Not all were eager to go; a couple of our wiser guys always sensed that we are not just going for a fun ride. Years of experience and countless mistakes provided us with sensible hints to orchestrate these trips, to make them less stressful as well as less "scentful."

The shot clinics in Albuquerque are always crowded with responsible pet owners, most of us arriving early so we can "hurry-up and patiently wait-in-line" with our dogs on leashes and cats in crates. Once we reach the tired and already-tested receptionist to register, our visit can become a comedy of errors.

New Mexico requires proof, for public health safety, of rabies vaccination. A rabies outbreak in our state is still a strong concern for our Department of Health officials. Statistics in 2012 revealed more than thirty-eight confirmed rabies cases, most of which were wildlife. But this report also revealed that it was necessary to euthanize thirty-two unvaccinated dogs, exposed to rabies.

In Albuquerque, we are proud of our HEART (Humane and Ethical Animal Rules and Treatment) city ordinance that requires that each pet has proof of current rabies inoculation, a permanent micro-chip number, a city license for present year and a certificate of spaying or neutering unless owner has secured an intact-animal permit, for which an annual assessment and additional fees are charged.

Excluding their medical records, our household of rescues accumulates four documents per pet, times nine to thirteen pets—almost a dissertation. Following the vaccinations is the confusing ordeal of matching the correct rabies certificate with the correct metal ID tag and, using pliers, attaching its "S-ring" to the collar of the matching pet. This chaotic pairing is repeated once again the following month, when each city pet license arrives, separately, by mail. Although we try for organization, our chaotic confusion would have made a great script for the Three Stooges.

The city-required multiple-permit for a household with

more than four dogs is an entirely different experience, requiring that a thorough walk-through be conducted in our home and around our property, yearly, by a competent and knowledgeable officer. What a relief that these challenging responsibilities take but a few days of each year! What a relief that we accept these to be a completely necessary experience to ensure the safety of "the guys"!

Wally and I are fortunate to have our loving and loveable pets protected by these local and state laws and ordinances. We are hoping for even stronger ordinances and laws that will better protect these precious animals. We are hoping for quicker intervention on behalf of Albuquerque's abandoned and abused pets. Add to our "hope" list the need for a greater number of compassionate homes to foster, adopt, and love these cast-away pets, unconditionally, as they accept us.

Although our family has decidedly improved the quality of life of these discarded dogs and cats, in return they have certainly enriched ours with their unquestioning acceptance and unselfish love. As each of our pets would pass "over the Rainbow Bridge," our grief for each loss was never lessened just because we had a houseful of remaining pets. Each pet has occupied his own special and unique place in our hearts. But, we were thankful that the time required for the care of our remaining dogs and cats gave us less time to dwell on the recent death of one of our cherished tails.

While we nourished their physical and emotional needs, their devotion in turn nourished our spiritual needs, making us into better, far richer people. What a reward! What a gift! If described in today's lingo, this would be termed a definite "win-win situation."

*Waterplay with Sinbad and Kate, 1943 Carlsbad, NM,
would soon cease.*

CHAPTER 2

WELCOME HOME?

"Cruelty against the defenseless is not defensible."

– C. E. Smyer

My very first dog, a dapper little black and white Boston Terrier was rescued by my father from a burning trash-barrel in a Borger, Texas alley. Because of the serious burns on his hind feet, his fur grew in cute, curly patches on both back feet. My parents named him Sinbad (after Sinbad the Sailor, vintage 1935). Sinbad was my adoring playmate, my constant companion.

A few months before the birth of my baby sister, Delia, in January, 1943, we had moved into our newly built home in Carlsbad, New Mexico. While Mother was still busy unpacking boxes, I would take one of her cookbooks (already unpacked), and read to Sinbad a pretend story, always about a girl and her dog. I was very proud that, because of the food pictures, I could always hold it right side up (or so I thought). I was almost four years old.

A month before our unforeseeable tragedy, I stand proudly with my newly-born sister, Delia.

My very special adventures with Sinbad came after our afternoon naps together in my new room. We would race to the grassed yard for our wonderful water games in my metal washtub-pool. My squeals of delight pierced the neighborhood on most warm days as he, hose in mouth, playfully squirted me. I was puzzled why, after a couple of hours of soggy activity, Mother would take us both into the house and fill the bathtub with more water to bathe me, no splashing, no Sinbad, just suds, soap, and a soft washcloth. She explained this bath away succinctly. "Don't you want to look special when your father comes home from work tonight?"

No more questions. No discussion necessary. I adored my father. After dinnertime my tall (6'3"), handsome daddy would take me in his arms; we would dance together and sing *Daisy, Daisy*. When he came home from working in the lab at the potash mines, Daddy, even though obviously tired, would quickly sketch any special animal on his specimen tags that I requested. He even drew Sinbad. I kept them all. But six weeks after my fourth birthday, on the first day of Spring in March, 1943, my family's life tragically changed forever.

My young and healthy, thirty-five-year-old father suddenly became gravely ill. Although he was hospitalized, his physicians were unable to diagnose the worsening condition in his lungs. Five anguishing days later, as I waited, frightened, outside his room holding a chocolate milkshake for him, Daddy died. My mother, aunts and uncles did not leave his room to explain to me what had happened. But a nurse quietly came out of his room, firmly took my hand, tossed the milk shake, and gently led me downstairs to the hospital waiting room. Mrs. Novett, the kind neighbor who was watching my two-month old sister, Delia, took me to her home for the evening. She didn't mention my mother or daddy, but it was obvious that something was seriously wrong.

Following this unexpected death of my loving and beloved father, our house was filled for days with solemn friends and family, consoling my grieving mother. My short four years had never experienced a death, so I couldn't fully understand what it meant. Why were all my aunts and uncles speaking in such hushed, comforting, tones? Their terms "passed", "gone", "in heaven" were dark, confusing, harsh, and too forever—kind-of like something you couldn't take back. They frightened me when they discussed an "open coffin," "burial site" or "an autopsy." This sober scene made me realize that death was really bad. It meant something grave had happened to my wonderful father. He probably would not ever leave that hospital. Death was something that made my mother's mood dark and despondent. It caused her sunny face to turn gray and drawn. Everyone seemed to be embracing, crying, dabbing at their eyes with a tissue.

I, too, was very sad and very frightened, but this was not the time to ask my questions. So, for those bleak and uncertain days, I became very quiet and simply clutched Sinbad as I wept and whispered into his pointed, perky ears.

Mother cared for Delia, only two months old, while she handled the funeral arrangements the required legalities and the burial of my father in the family's cemetery plot in Roswell, NM, seventy-eight miles to the north. After listing our newly built home with a real estate representative, she organized the tedious and permanent move for the three of us, 185 miles north to Grandaddy's house in Riley's Switch, New Mexico, into the very house where she grew up. She considered me to be too young to attend or to understand Daddy's funeral, so her middle sister, Aunt Fey, unsympathetic and inconvenienced by my father's death, accompanied me on a quiet, somber and rainy train ride to my new home in Riley's Switch. This small railroading, ranching and farming community, located only seven miles from the Texas border, was the fourth largest in a sparsely populated state of less than 600,000.

As soon as our train pulled into the station, I could hardly wait for the conductor to unload my Sinbad from his metal cage in the separate luggage car. As we pushed open the huge and heavy wooden door to my new home, I was greeted with a much-needed, long-lasting hug by my special granddaddy. I melted in his arms and softly cried. It was relief for me that our emotionally racked family would be welcomed into the home of such a generous, wise and kind man. Recently retired as Superintendent of the Pecos Division of the Atchison Topeka and Santa Fe Railroad (AT&SF RR), he was one of the best-known railway officials in the Southwest. Because his job was the railroad and had been since 1887, he was always eager to take Mother and me on trips in his private car on "his choo-train." Voilá! He was my ChooDaddy, seventy-two years old, mostly bald, 5'8", but an imposing, dignified figure in his three-piece Hickey Freeman suits. His very presence seemed to signify stability and integrity.

Aunt Fey, her husband, Uncle Clem, and their two nine-year-old adopted twins also lived with ChooDaddy along with Aunt Martha, the eldest of mother's sisters. Choo-Daddy held me high in his arms while I slowly assessed my new family and my new home. Although my tiny, well-groomed Mother was only five feet tall, she was inches taller than her two older sisters and didn't look like them at all. Mother's long wavy auburn hair was always fashionably styled, and her flawless skin and beautiful nose were show-stoppers. In sharp contrast were Aunt Martha's dark features, disheveled appearance and her dazed, empty look. Aunt Fey's manly haircut did not soften her angular, angry features. Her distrustful nature and demanding voice made her appear to be uncompromising and unaccommodating.

Her bearded husband, Uncle Clem, tall and large framed, wore a sour expression as if an offensive odor lingered in the air. His glaring eyes and pursed lips reflected his displeasure that his wife had traveled to Carlsbad to bring me back on the train. Their twins, my cousins Ralph and Rhonda, didn't say a word; they just stared, dumbfounded. They hadn't the foggiest idea of what to make of Sinbad and me. Wasn't anyone but ChooDaddy happy to see me?

This was my new 'home sweet home'…but was it?

My new home, ChooDaddy's, was large, warm and comfortable, but the welcoming was cool and intimidating. To ease my obvious discomfort, ChooDaddy said he would make an exception to his usual house rules. Sinbad and I could sleep in his room until Mother and Delia arrived from Carlsbad. ChooDaddy sat in his wicker rocker next to our bed and transformed his nimble fingers into awesome hand-shadows while telling amazing stories about dogs, all of which he swore happened to him as a boy in North Carolina. This quieted some of the anxiety I was feeling about my confusing reception by Mother's family.

Once Mother and Delia arrived a month later, the atmosphere in the house cooled rapidly and became even more uncomfortable for everyone. It was distressing that Aunt Fey was so openly disapproving of my mother, a grudge which had festered between these sisters for decades. Now the two sisters were forced to live together again, this time with families of their own. Aunt Fey made no pretention of welcoming Mother home. She was certainly neither gracious nor accepting of the sudden intrusion into her home-life by Mother, Delia, Sinbad and me. Our move necessitated quite an upheaval: big changes in living quarters, routines, responsibilities and relationships for each of us.

Most difficult of all, ChooDaddy demanded the surface healing of these ugly sibling wounds opened years ago between rivaling sisters. I listened, confused, as a stern ChooDaddy I had never seen before stated these unconditional house-rules to both women. "The schism must heal. All past sins are to be forgotten and forgiven. Present inconveniences should to be taken in stride. Compatibility and respect must reign within the confines of my home. Eileen and her family have just lost a husband and a father, so they are to be treated, for these first, few months at least, with kid gloves."

What a frightening change for a suddenly alone child! My adoring, playful father was gone, and my wonderful, cheerful mother was gone, too, all day, as it was now necessary that she attend business school to learn clerical skills. Her liberal college education at St. Mary's of Notre Dame and University of Colorado would certainly not land her a job with the AT&SF RR, Riley's Switch's largest employer.

When she did return from school, she always seemed to disappear into her bedroom. I could see her crying and would offer her my Sinbad to hold and pet. His constant presence and love had certainly calmed and consoled me as we both adjusted to this new and strange environment. Instead, as throughout her thirty-one years, her loving and dependable father was there, trying to ease her heart-wrenching agony. Time would soften the sharpest edges of her pain and loneliness, but she desperately missed my father for the rest of her increasingly difficult life. She never re-married, explaining that, just as with her father, she had been "blessed to have had the best."

I had hoped I would be able to spend my days with my understanding ChooDaddy, but now he, too, had a new and time-consuming responsibility—to care for my newly born two-month-old sister, Delia while Mother was attending school. After Grandmother's death in 1925, he became the tender caregiver for his oldest daughter, Aunt Martha, whose severe skull injury at birth in 1901, resulted in permanent brain damage, making her completely dependent.

ChooDaddy had his hands full as the daytime guardian of both a two-month-old and a mentally-disabled daughter. His time was taken.

What a lost soul I was! Sinbad and I spent hours every day wandering aimlessly, not daring to explore this unfamiliar home inhabited by so many unfamiliar, unfriendly relatives. On weekends, Mother, who suffered a severe limp from polio as a child, slowly walked me around my new neighborhood to scope out the territory. With Sinbad on a red cloth leash (which was actually Mother's belt), we three walked several blocks in every direction, only to discover that this neighborhood was inhabited solely by retirees. There was no evidence of any other small children. That was okay. I had Sinbad, and ChooDaddy's home had a sizeable, landscaped yard where we two could play. His large trees, planted in 1921, provided plenty of shade from New Mexico's bright sun.

A month later, Mother and I were very concerned when we had to take Sinbad to the vet for an ear infection. In the years before our move to Riley's Switch, both of my ears had been lanced many times; I remembered the intense pain followed by the soothing relief that came from a hot-water bottle. While waiting, early one unseasonably cold and windy May evening, for Mother's return from school, I chose to sit with Sinbad, close to the living room fireplace, hoping its heat would help his earache. Suddenly, Ralph, my cousin, rushed up to also warm himself at the fire. But his quick movements must have caused the ring on his finger to come off and fall on the hearth rug where we were sitting. Sinbad started to chomp on this shiny new object.

Angrily, Ralph kicked Sinbad directly on his infected ear.

In retaliation, Sinbad growled and bit his hand. Although it did not break his skin, experiencing a dog bite is very frightening (especially if you are just a kid). Ralph, of course, yelled out loudly and ran to kitchen to fetch his father, who roughly scooped-up my Sinbad, and quickly took him out the back door. It all happened too quickly. No one even asked any questions. With an intimidating glare that dared me to question her authority Aunt Fey tightly grabbed me by the arm and pulled me to my room.

As she tried to close the door to my bedroom, I argued. I was desperate; I pleaded. "You weren't even in the room when it happened. You and Uncle Clem knew that my Sinbad had a bad ear. Ralph didn't mean to kick his sore ear. Sinbad just reacted to the pain. He is only a little dog. Please don't hurt him."

She gave me a censorious frown, daring me to speak again. Then Aunt Fey forcefully closed the door. No one paid any attention to me. I was devastated! There were no explanations. My uncertainty and fear were so intense that they actually produced such physical pain in my tummy that I ran to the bathroom, my stomach racked with spasms and vomiting.

Almost an hour later, Mother returned home with ChooDaddy. Before she could even close the back door, I was in her arms and sobbing uncontrollably. I couldn't catch my breath and was even choking as I tried to explain what happened with Sinbad, but Aunt Fey and Uncle Clem were telling it differently.

I knew it was wrong to interrupt an adult but this time it was critical. Raising my small voice so I could be heard over their incorrect explanations, I kept repeating, "They took my Sinbad. What did they do to him? Where is my Sinbad?"

Mother became very emotional, her tone of voice quivering. ChooDaddy shook his head and tried to calm both Mother and me. Motioning Uncle Clem and Mother outside, he followed them from the room, therefore ending my witness to their heated discussion about my Sinbad. I never saw my best-bud again. Sinbad's name was never mentioned again for years, except by me. I always remembered him in my prayers.

It was to be more than ten years later before I was made aware that, because of his actions that evening, Uncle Clem had been reprimanded by his supervisor at AT&SF RR. An animal-cruelty complaint had been filed by ChooDaddy. I also learned that Uncle Clem had snapped Sinbad's neck and his body had been tossed in the trash barrel in our alley… sadly like the barrel in Borger, TX, whence he came.

The displeasure between Mother and Aunt Fey became worse. For years I watched as ChooDaddy tried patiently to ride herd on this deteriorating situation, interfering only when absolutely necessary to keep the peace. Patience and compromise were required skills for the nine of us residing in his home. Mother made repeated attempts throughout those years, imploring her sister to forgive her, to mend the broken fences. But these pleas for healing fell on deaf ears.

Mother's final request came thirty-two years later, in June 1975, when, complications from a previous March surgery required that she be admitted to the intensive-care unit of Albuquerque's AT&SF RR Memorial Hospital. Knowing that she had but a few hours left to live, Mother urgently pleaded with me to locate Aunt Fey, who, as fate would have it, was in town attending a national convention at a nearby hotel in Old Town. I prevailed upon Aunt Fey to come with me to the hospital. While they spoke, alone, in hushed tones in Mother's hospital room, I waited outside her room and prayed fervently for the entire twenty minutes that they reach a peaceful solution, a solution that would be good for our families. It was to no avail. Their schism was not laid to rest. Mother's final effort was in vain.

The "why" remains an unanswered question. Regretfully, those not-to-be-forgotten injustices (imagined or real) would influence and cloud the attitudes and actions of our family relationships for generations to follow.

Chapter 3

DOGNAPPING

"Dogs are not our whole life, but they make our life whole."

– Roger Caras

In response to Sinbad's ugly death, my behavior changed for the worse. Except for the constant flow of tears, I became too quiet, unresponsive, uncommunicative, even around Mother and ChooDaddy. Mother hoped that sending me to kindergarten, one block away, would take my mind off my Sinbad and fill my lonely hours by meeting and playing with other children my own age. She never envisioned that I would choose instead to become a fairly accomplished dognapper. She wanted me to make friends, and indeed I did: with the long haired, black-and-white Collie who lived next door to my kindergarten.

Each morning as his owners left for work, they tied him, on a short rope, to a tree on their front lawn. Cruel students from the kindergarten and the elementary school across the street taunted and teased him with long sticks and rocks on their way both to and from school and even during recess hours. My own intervention in his behalf only found me ridiculed and often at the wrong end of their sticks, with a few scratches and cuts of my own, too.

Day after day teachers and students had observed these kids abusing this restrained, defenseless dog, and yet no one interceded and stopped it. When I precociously queried their lack of concern, I was told, in an authoritative voice, "Go home. They are not hurting *your* dog. This is not your business." I might have only been four years old, but I definitely knew better. ChooDaddy had said that hurting was everyone's business. My heart ached!

Their inhumane behavior should not be allowed to continue, but what could I do? I could easily run home to get ChooDaddy, but what if Aunt Fey was there instead? She really disliked me, and who knew what she would do? If ChooDaddy wasn't present to help me, she was a force to be reckoned with. I was definitely intimidated and very fearful of any possible encounter with her.

What to do? What to do? I was so frightened that it was hard to clear my mind to think of anything to do, anywhere, any way to help this dog that would not involve others. For almost a week (it seemed like forever), I had been saying my prayers, but no help, as yet, for the poor dog.

My simplistic four-year-old mind could only devise a very simple solution. I ditched kindergarten, untied his rope and took my new black-and-white friend (I named him Riley.) to my new home across the street, where I petted and quietly played with him all day on the south side of our large back yard. The south side held an unattached one-bedroom home, the daytime sleeping-quarters for Uncle Clem, an AT&SF RR engineer at night. During the day, no one ventured into that part of the yard, so he would have quiet to sleep.

Happiness was a dog named Riley. I was careful each

afternoon to return him to his home in plenty of time, before his owners would return from work. Tying him back to that tree, I felt like a traitor to my new friend!

Even though this routine continued from October until May, I was never sure why no one at the kindergarten reported my absence. However, I was to be found out and punished for my blatant dognapping. As usual, Riley and I had played and fallen asleep on the backyard lawn, only to be awakened when ChooDaddy whispered in my ear, "Miss Kate, I am very disappointed with you."

Whoops! Up I bolted to find the owners of Riley, glaring down at me. I thought they would be happy that I brought him to my home where he was safe and couldn't be teased, but they were shouting, threatening and shaking their fingers at me. They angrily forbade me to ever pet or play with their dog again, and ChooDaddy assured them that I would abide by their request. All I had wanted to do was to keep Riley safe and happy.

The school was almost over; maybe Riley would be all right.

Both very displeased with my behavior, Mother and ChooDaddy lectured me about taking anything that did not belong to me, even an animal I felt was being abused. I did not understand; I did not agree, but I dared not say a word. I just listened and cried.

Our family was surprised that evening by a phone call from Riley's owner. He and his wife had been very upset about when they discovered this recently developed situation with me and their dog. There were no fences around the property of this rented home. They had no other place to keep their dog except tied to that sole tree in their front yard. So, because of my unsupervised actions, he had been forced to kill Riley with his rifle.

ChooDaddy phoned a security officer for AT&SF, but evidently no laws had been broken. *What a sad, harsh world, especially for doggies!* I wept uncontrollably, trying to grapple with my responsibility in this needless tragedy and its resulting and violent cessation of life. My small body was heaved with sobs of guilt. The horror of their retribution (or was it revenge?) devastated me.

Within just a few months, I had lost my father, whom I cherished, and two dogs whom I also treasured. I was in a new home with no friends. Because they were needed elsewhere, no one could take the time to care for me during the day. So I tried to develop an independent attitude. I continued to ditch kindergarten and instead wandered daily up and down the neighborhood streets with no pattern, no destination, ringing doorbells, searching for dogs to walk, pet or hold. Because most of the families in ChooDaddy's neighborhood were, like him, retired, the few homes that did have dogs also had older, live-in grandchildren, whose responsibility it was to walk their dogs.

Again I was busted, but by a well-intentioned neighbor, who for my own safety reported me to Mother and Choo-Daddy for roaming the neighborhood alone. My mother, still grieving and stressed, patiently explained, "Kate, you are much too young to go wandering, by yourself, around the neighborhood. Everyone at home is too occupied with their many responsibilities to take you on your walks, and I am still busy with school, completing my classes. Please, consider this and work harder to adjust. This situation is difficult for everyone."

Mother proposed a solution for my new state of unhappiness and loneliness. Since I definitely did not wish to return to kindergarten, I could spend my days, while she was gone, with my father's sister, another aunt, Aunt Stella, who had no children of her own. She and Uncle Joe lived only two blocks away in the first house ChooDaddy built in Riley's Switch.

They were cheerful and sympathetic and most important of all, they had time for me. They helped quiet my hunger for attention. She delighted in baking me a variety of delicious cookies, even allowing me to roll the dough and cut the shapes into doggies. Aunt Stella read me storybooks, taught me songs, while Uncle Joe concocted wonderful tales of Superman, SuperDog and his sidekick, Squirt. These inventive names of that team came from Uncle Joe's active imagination. He thoughtfully added dogs to any story he was reading to me and made sure there were happy endings. Their energies were even successful in keeping me off the neighborhood streets in my quest for dogs. Their comfy home, their genuine interest in me and their acts of kindness were my first tastes of normalcy in the recent, agonizingly painful months of change.

Even though they didn't have any pets, Aunt Stella taught me a special prayer just for dogs. "Dear God, I am my doggie's world. Help me to keep him safe. Amen."

Within a year, Uncle Joe's position as chief engineer for the Pecos Division, AT&SF Railroad, earned him a career move, chief engineer for the Western Lines, in Amarillo, Texas, 100 miles to the east. He would later author the book *From Cab To Caboose, Fifty Years of Railroading.*

We had been in Riley's Switch only seventeen months

and had tried various ideas for childcare. Once my Aunt Stella and Uncle Joe moved, Mother had no more back-up plans for my care. She could not leave me at home with my busy ChooDaddy, who was already responsible for Delia and Aunt Martha. Nor would Aunt Fey watch me. Fudging on my age, Mother enrolled me that August, 1944, in the first grade at Eugene Field Elementary, across the street.

Mother became very serious as she explained to me that I would have to be a good student so they would allow me to stay, and I would have to do everything my teacher asked. I had no other choice. I had no other place to go so I took my school work seriously; and, after difficult months of adjustment, I finally excelled as a student. Still I was withdrawn, very lonely and didn't make many friends at school. When my first grade teacher, Mrs. Johnson, brought this to the attention of my mother, I explained that when I had my very own dog, he would be my very best companion and playmate.

But because of cousin Ralph's fear of dogs (supposedly due to the Sinbad incident) and his possible allergies to dog dander (not tested by their physician), Mother's answer was, "Not now, Kate. Everyone in the family is trying hard to make this work. Please be patient and wait until your aunt, uncle and cousins move from here to a home of their own."

Now I knew exactly what to ask for in my prayers at Friday's Benediction service and Sunday's Mass at Sacred Heart Catholic Church. For the next five years, I was most fervent in reciting the rosary as well as my morning, noon and evening prayers. And, in the fifth grade those prayers were answered.

Sandy and Li'l Abe, mother and son:
Beware of neighbors bearing gifts.

CHAPTER 4

SANDY'S SURPRISE

"For an animal person, an animal-less home is no home at all."

– <u>The Cat Who Came For Christmas</u>
Cleveland Amory

The summer before the fifth grade, my aunt, uncle and cousins finally realized their dream of building a home and moved to the Denver, Colorado area. The stress level in my small life was lessened considerably, and my hope for a pet dog rose to new heights. To make sure that I was not hitching my star to a mirage, I reviewed our family's attitude concerning dog-ownership.

Aunt Martha was always stopping to pet and talk to neighborhood dogs. I was sure that ChooDaddy enjoyed dogs because hanging above his bookcase was this beautiful framed painting, about eighteen inches wide by two-feet tall, of an aging Border Collie at the foot of his elderly master. Under the painting was a matching, larger frame in which was printed the lengthy prose *The Last Will and Testament of an Extremely Distinguished Dog*, written in the early 1940's by Eugene O'Neill, an American playwright and Nobel laureate in literature. Often, ChooDaddy would read chosen stanzas of this long but touching ode to us before our afternoon naps and evening bedtime. Although it is written under the authorship of his dog, Silverdene Emblem O'Neill (Blemis), its sentiment was touching, reaching out particularly to all who have lost a pet. And its humor would awaken smiles in all manipulated and pliant dog-owned humans. It is definitely a must read for all pet owners.

With the hailed departure of Aunt Fey, Uncle Clem, Ralph and his twin sister, Rhonda, I became certain that a dog would be Mother's perfect surprise Christmas gift for me. However, we were unable to celebrate our first anticipated Christmas together, just the five of us in Choo-Daddy's home. Mother suffered a stroke the last week in

November and was hospitalized in Albuquerque through the month of December. After Mother returned from the hospital, only four weeks until my birthday, I began devising new pet-getting strategies, accompanied by a multitude of poorly disguised hints.

"We have a visiting pottery teacher in art class. I think I will make a dog bowl."

"We must practice putting our shoes away at night, so once we have a dog, he will not be tempted to chew on them," I cautioned.

As we sat down for dinner, I began the conversation. "I got an 'A' yesterday on my book report, *Beautiful Joe* by Margaret Marshall Saunders. It's a classic, published in 1893. Its author chose to present it as an autobiography, from the point of view of an abused mixed-breed dog named Beautiful Joe. Have you ever read it, Mother?"

So much for the obvious. My February birthday passed without even the slightest mention of a dog. Instead Mother gave me a tent, a really nice, roomy tent, but… not a dog. To put it mildly, I was terribly disappointed but never defeated. I decided to tenaciously breach the subject a week later, a date when my mother would be home early for dinner, where we all were encouraged, as we sat around the dinner table, to share our day's happenings and our concerns.

That morning, I was heavy in thought about a new strategy to approach this subject…again. I sauntered into my fifth-grade room just as a classmate, JoAnn, was complaining that her father, a pharmacist, felt that their family dog was getting fat, gaining too much weight, and costing too much money. JoAnn was saddened by his decision to abandon their dog by the railroad tracks this evening. I tried to console her and to get more information.

The cruelty and callousness of the situation was shocking! This is wrong. I know we can save this dog's life. I had to let ChooDaddy know before something bad happened to that dog. Waiting for the school bell, I fidgeted and danced in my classroom seat all morning as if I had ants in my pants.

Finally, when we were released at noon for lunch, I raced home, across the street, and breathlessly relayed JoAnn's brutal description to ChooDaddy, who listened with quiet and solemn interest. Within minutes, he was on the phone to JoAnn's father, confirming the inhumane proposal and demanding that the "fat" dog be made ready for our family to adopt when we arrived at their home early that evening. Aunt Martha walked to a nearby family grocers, Hubby's, for dog food while I returned to school.

The wait was interminable. *Who could study? Who could eat supper? Did we really have to wash all the dinner dishes first?* I was more excited than I had been in years. *Maybe we could save this dog and maybe we would finally have a dog— again—for real!*

Our black Studebaker was packed with Mother, Choo-Daddy, Aunt Martha, Delia and me. When we arrived, JoAnn's father signed a paper prepared by ChooDaddy's attorney, and the "fat" dog had a new home that didn't care if she was "fat"—ours. My young sister removed her brown leather belt from her jeans, using it as both collar and leash. Back out to the car we pranced, danced and sang, tears freely flowing from our eyes. She was beautiful, this small blonde dog of no discernible breed. And, indeed she was very heavy, but captivated us with those beautiful, big hazel eyes and the long tail that never ceased wagging. It was as if she knew why we were there: that now she was our dog. Because of her color, Delia and I cleverly chose the name Sandy.

Her bed, a pillow covered with a flour sack, was placed under the kitchen sink. Aunt Martha made sure that her water and food bowls were full. Delia and I wanted to sleep next to her all night, but our family assured us that she would be safe. In the early morning hours, there were noisy and unusual sounds coming from the kitchen. Sensing some kind of crisis, I awakened Delia and jumped out of bed with one scary thought: *Had something happened to our Sandy?*

ChooDaddy, still in his three-piece suit, was kneeling on the floor over Sandy's bed and Mother was carrying a large pot of water from the stove. There were lots of extra towels strewn everywhere. With a finger over her lips, Mother signaled our silence. We watched in amazement as ChooDaddy helped Sandy to deliver five wet puppies.

Because today was February 12, it was easy to name the first four blond puppies: Linc, Abraham, Li'l Abe, and Cupid. Delia immediately chose the only black puppy, proudly naming him Fido.

ChooDaddy explained that he was moving Sandy with her pups to his bedroom so he could watch-over them until we could find good homes for them.

Whatttt? I was hoping we could keep all her puppies. This selfish thought almost deprived me of getting my one puppy, Li'l Abe.

From that day until her death eight years later, Sandy and ChooDaddy were almost inseparable. She slept in his bedroom (on a feather bed), was hand-fed from a sterling spoon and drank from a china bowl. She accompanied him on his daily visits to the bank, and, of course, she was always situated in a strategic position, at his feet, as he prepared meals…just in case a morsel dropped to the floor.

Several months later Sandy and all of her pups were spayed and neutered. ChooDaddy had very strict beliefs about how to respect life and our planet Earth.

One was population control of all of God's creatures, including people.

I overheard ChooDaddy mention to Mother, "The veterinarian bill for her spaying was forwarded to JoAnn's irresponsible father. If he does not honor his financial responsibility in this matter, I will have a security officer from AT&SF RR speak to him, since his shamelessly inhumane intentions were to leave Sandy near their tracks, an action which could have been a very dangerous one for passengers and personnel on a train."

I was ecstatic, in another world, lost in puppy love with Li'l Abe. Was he ever darling with his medium length, white wavy fur! A whisper of a golden spot over his eye and another at the tip of his overactive long tail added to his appeal.

Happy to see me when I returned from school and quick to learn tricks, Li'l Abe was also the confidant for all of my little-girl secrets. All girls of all ages have secrets, secrets they must share. And how we delighted in one another! He was such a good-natured little guy, who, slept, of course, under the kitchen sink, but shared summer naps with me under our large apple tree in the beautiful back yard. When I finally put up my new birthday tent that summer, we spent our whole evenings together, sleeping on basement blankets, unaware and uncaring of the uneven and cold ground, dotted with occasional sharp stones. *Who cared?*

While I was engrossed in Sandy and Li'l Abe, my sister, Delia, was collecting her own menagerie of discarded animals. Stray cats that roamed our neighborhood now were fed safely inside our walled yard. To save the lives of those unsold pastel colored chickens and bunnies sold by five and dime stores at Easter, she brought them home. We built rabbit hutches and chicken coops.

Delia leashes Sandy for neighborhood walk.

Our family will always remember one particular bunny, which Mother purchased at Easter-time, 1949, for Delia. Already dyed green by Woolworth Department Store, the rabbit defied the normal three-week life expectancy for chemically-dyed animals. Delia, remembering the cute bunny in Disney's movie, *Bambi*, named him Thumper (King Kong would have been more appropriate.). He and Delia would actually play in the back yard, where our dogs totally ignored him, giving him a wide berth. Once he reached adulthood, he was coal black and weighed more than twenty-three pounds. Delia entered him in the annual Curry County Fair where, for three consecutive years, he was awarded the Best Buck certificate and blue ribbon. His rabbit room was the empty tool shed attached to our insulated garage, which was located about ninety feet from the back door of the house. When any of us would arrive after dark and walk from the garage to the house, Thumper would dash out of his quarters and hiss loudly at us, sometimes lunging at our ankles. His attacks were really scary! We were whirling, darting and dashing to avoid his sharp little teeth. Since having polio as a child, Mother was not sturdy on her feet, and escaping Thumper was pretty stressful for her.

Finally, our patient ChooDaddy put his foot down. "Delia, Thumper's aggression can no longer be tolerated. Ask your best friend, Carlene if Thumper could possibly visit and socialize with some of the bunnies on her farm. It might improve his mood."

After four weeks of socializing on the Stovall farm, a mild and friendly Thumper returned. What a welcome change! ChooDaddy was correct. Socializing was the answer. Two weeks later, the consequence of socializing resulted in Best Buck Thumper giving birth to six black bunnies. "Everyone, including the Curry County Fair judges, thought he was a buck," was the humorous explanation of ChooDaddy and Delia. From three months of age, rabbits can become pregnant, giving birth to four to eight babies almost every thirty days.

Today my sister's Oak City, NC, farm is home to numerous horses, donkeys, cows, pigs, chickens, rabbits, cats and dogs, all of them named, all treated with tenderness and respect. She does not consider these animals to be a labor of love, but her friends, and thus her privilege. ChooDaddy was correct in his character assessment. "If it breathes, Delia will respect, love and care for it."

By her sixth year in Riley's Switch, Delia and Fido had found many friends her age in our neighborhood, all of whom had moved in recently with their grandparents. One afternoon, while they were hard at play in the front yard, Li'l Abe and I were playing ball in the back yard. I was startled to see, standing at the gate, our elderly neighbor, Mrs. Gidding, with her small, irritable white dog, Little One, a Chihuahua-Terrier cross. She had brought some raw liver slices for our dogs.

What a kind, neighborly gesture!

When she tossed the liver over our wall, Li'l Abe hungrily scarfed it all down, saving none for Sandy. Because of this, her life would be spared. Sandy lived only because she was not spry enough to catch the thrown meat.

When I returned from walking the friendly neighbor and her unfriendly dog back to her home, across the alley, and thanking her, Li'l Abe was behaving very strangely, and suddenly started to run amok in circles, panting, crying, until he fell into the grass, unmoving. I grabbed Sandy and ran inside for ChooDaddy, but it was too late. Li'l Abe lay dead; his agony had ended. I cried out and grabbed my midsection, feeling actual physical pain. The emotional trauma left my mind in shock, my body in spasms. His horrific death is embedded in my memory.

The only food I had seen him digest was the liver from our neighbor.

What perverse pleasure could killing my innocent puppy bring to this woman?

My immediate reaction was to accuse this elderly woman of poisoning Li'l Abe. ChooDaddy crossed the alley separating our homes with quick strides. But then he hesitated, and instead of knocking on Mrs. Gidding's door, he crossed the street to the home of her dutiful son, a local businessman. Because of her age, he felt it more prudent to speak with her son. Having set the facts forward concerning L'il Abe's convulsions and death, ChooDaddy also mentioned that he was very concerned with the poisoned food being so close to the front yard, where small children played unaware.

No guilt was established. Nothing was resolved. There was no evidence, just the observation of a fifth-grader. I had once again, in a tragic, violent and intentional manner, lost my beloved dog, my most cherished friend.

I was now ten years old, angry, emotional and brave enough to challenge my ChooDaddy. Our family's tradition, every evening at dinner time, was for each of us, by seating order, to explain what deed we had performed that day to make our world a better world. No one was exempt from this custom; all of us participated: ChooDaddy, Aunt Martha, Mother, Delia and I. It was ironic that in the previous month, during one of these dinnertime revelations, I had mentioned what my deed had been: walking our elderly neighbor, Mrs. Gidding, and her intense dog across the street so she could visit her son.

That evening, when it was my time to speak, it was again to be about Mrs. Gidding, but in an entirely different context. So overcome with both grief and anger, I hadn't ChooDaddy's required disclosure, but I certainly had a question, "Why wouldn't a good deed be putting an unusually cruel individual in jail for killing a defenseless animal? Wouldn't that be a deterrent for others who hurt animals? That's stealing a life." You could have heard a pin drop. The silence was interminable.

ChooDaddy gave me a stern, but not totally disapproving look. "Let me raise new questions. Each of you should ponder them so we can discuss your answers tomorrow evening. Would bringing animal-cruelty charges against a seventy-year-old woman solve anything? Would it bring back the life of Li'l Abe? Would it not cause her son and his family unnecessary grief and brand them with a stigma for something over which they had no control? Do you have clinical proof that her liver slices were the cause of L'il Abe's death?" ChooDaddy had hard questions which he wanted each of us to ponder.

The next evening dinner session brought a variety of neither pat nor acceptable answers for his thought-provoking questions from our five family members.

"You should never accuse someone of any act without hard evidence."

"Current New Mexico laws were not written to protect pets."

"Children are not responsible for the actions of their parents."

It would be almost sixty years later, 1999, before laws establishing extreme cruelty to animals as a felonious offense in New Mexico would pass with votes from both our House and Senate, establishing the New Mexico Felony Animal-Cruelty Law of 1999, Chapter 107, as follows:

"An act relating to animals; increasing criminal penalties for cruelty to animals; providing for seizure of animals; providing criminal penalties for injury to or harassment of a police dog, police horse or fire dog; repealing and enacting sections of the NMSA 1978. Be it enacted by the legislature of the State of New Mexico: *continued on next page*

Section 1.

> *Section 30-18-1 NMSA 1978 (being Laws 1963, Chapter 303, Section 18-1) is repealed and a new Section 30-18-1 NMSDA 1978 is enacted to read:*

> *"30-18-1. Cruelty to animals-extreme cruelty to animals-penalties-exceptions.*

E. *Extreme cruelty to animals consists of a person:*

(1) *intentionally or maliciously torturing, mutilating, injuring or poisoning an animal; or*

(2) *maliciously killing an animal.*

F. *Whoever commits extreme cruelty to animals is guilty of a fourth degree felony and shall be sentenced pursuant to the provisions of Section 31-18-15 NMSA 1978.*

G. *The court may order a person convicted for committing cruelty to animals to participate in an animal-cruelty prevention program or an animal-cruelty education program. The court may also order a person convicted for committing cruelty to animals or extreme cruelty to animals to obtain psychological counseling for treatment of a mental health disorder if, in the court's judgment, the mental health disorder contributed to the commission of the criminal offense. The offender shall bear the expense of participating in an animal-cruelty prevention program, animal-cruelty education program or psychological counseling ordered by the court."*

This new law established animal cruelty (vs. extreme animal cruelty) as a misdemeanor on the first, second and third offense. It does not become a fourth-degree felony, like extreme animal cruelty, until the fourth offense. Animal cruelty, as defined in the present bill, includes negligently mistreating, injuring, tormenting or killing without lawful justification an animal. It also includes abandoning or failing to provide necessary sustenance to an animal under that individual's custody or control.

Animal activists in America have a strong advocacy. More U.S. households have pets than children. Joining forces with shelter directors, they continued to voice their concerns over New Mexico's weak animal-cruelty laws and the continuing and blatant animal abuse resulting. They cited New Mexico's weak and almost non-existent animal-cruelty laws and the state's ranking, by the animal legal defense fund, in "the worst five states for animals" category. Their demands for stronger laws were backed by numerous psychological, sociological and criminology studies and statistics, that animal abuse is a precursor to child abuse and domestic violence. Not only improving the lives of animals but also those of victims of domestic and child abuse, better-written, stronger and better enforced laws would increase the quality of life throughout our state.

During the 2011 legislative session, a stronger bill, New Mexico House Bill 319, was introduced by Rep. Al Park, making reckless mistreatment (abandoning, beating, poisoning, starving) of an animal a fourth-degree felony, and requiring those convicted to undergo psychological counseling. Present at this voting session was a canine lobbyist, three-legged Trinity, an American Bulldog who lost her leg to animal cruelty. Her presence served as a living reminder to our voting legislators of the abusive behavior encountered by so many pets in New Mexico. Still, entrusted with this knowledge and the future safety of many of our children and pets, the bill did not pass. No other legislation was proposed to take its place.

New Mexico's first 2013 legislative session introduced another excellent bill to strengthen those 1999 existing animal-cruelty laws and to better protect animals from extreme cruelty and neglect. It did not pass. Who were our New Mexico legislators listening to?

All states in America have differing animal-cruelty laws. Forty-seven, including New Mexico, designate some forms of cruelty punishable as but a fourth-degree felony. The key to that sentence is "some forms of cruelty." Is that acceptable… "some"? Will it provide sufficient protection for our companion animals? Is the punishment established by your state a strong enough deterrent? Is it enforceable?

My ChooDaddy, C.E. Smyer,
skillfully calmed our tumultuous household.

Chapter 5

HEARTBREAK

"The dog is the only animal on Earth who loves you more than he loves himself."

– Josh Billings

Although Sandy had adopted ChooDaddy completely, she was often in the company of either my sister (with Fido) or me during the summer. After the poisoning of Li'l Abe, when we would play with her or Fido, we were careful to never let them stay unattended in our walled-in back yard. And now we were constantly conducting thorough sweeps of our yard for foreign substances.

In three long-forgotten steamer trunks of Grandmother's in the basement, Delia and I discovered an array of flowing, dusty fabrics to make Sandy and Fido an assortment of costumes, which we custom-fitted with safety pins. Once their designer wardrobes were completed, we proudly entered both pets, sporting bonnets and petticoats, in floats for the well-attended annual Pioneer Days parade held in Riley's Switch.

Our productions covered all seasons. Because she would wear her outrageously large clown hat

Delia, Fido and I, busy actors, pose after our Sunday matinee.

and she would jump through hoops (held very low), Sandy was given the star role in our summer backyard circus. A dismantled apple basket provided a large enough hoop.

Fido and Delia pranced around wearing basement-designed costumes from *Deary Dot and Her Dog*, one of Mother's childhood books, circa 1919.

For our elaborate neighborhood Christmas musicals, presented yearly, Sandy wore Grandmother's filmy white curtains bunched into a multi-layered angel's robe and tied with her leash. Bone stays made perfect halos. Light from an open closet door framed their performances of holiday songs, skits and poetry.

Providing the background music were thick, black, ten-inch, 75 RPM Christmas records, scratchy-sounding from dust and years of use, and played on a self-winding record player. Programs were hand-written on the blank side of last year's received Christmas cards. Admission was one penny. We were already into recycling seventy years ago!

Assuming the part of her agents, we convinced our music and drama teachers to include a bit part in their upcoming plays and operettas for an aging, calm and adorable canine. A star was born! Fido, still an active puppy, had too much energy to be bothered with the demands of an actor's life.

We had our own loving dog, Sandy, who had become an integral and loved member of our family. However, I could not help being overwhelmed by distress whenever I would encounter any abandoned dog because Riley's Switch did not have a humane shelter. More than sixty years later, statistics from their city-operated shelter, which is under the direction of the police department, reveal a euthanasia rate exceeding sixty-eight percent. Sundance Ranch Sanctuary and Hope Defined Animal Rescue work diligently to promote adoptions in that New Mexico area.

Throughout my three years at Marshall Junior High School, I found and brought home a motley crew of wandering dogs, all sizes, all ages, haggard, painfully thin with dull, dirty coats. Most had infestations of either fleas or ticks. They were without collars or identification. After Delia and I gave them a Joy Suds bath outside in our metal tub, ChooDaddy would take them to our veterinarian for inoculations, treatments and the always necessary spaying or neutering.

ChooDaddy stated that we would be allowed to keep them only if their owners did not respond to the ads we wrote for *Riley's Switch News Journal* classifieds or to the hand-printed flyers we posted around town. Although we tacked our signs to wooden fences, trees, telephone poles and doors of businesses, we never received a single inquiry about any of our "found dogs." Sixty-three years later, New Mexico's "found dogs" are still too numerous and too much in need of homes.

Current photos of New Mexico's pound pups are posted to stimulate adoptions. PHOTOS BY JOYCE FAY

All, without exception, were friendly, appreciative, quiet dogs, who stayed in newly built backyard doghouses, situated on the side yard away from the fences and sidewalks. With the help of our neighbors, classmates and a local veterinarian, we found new, responsible and loving owners for each one. But even though we had taken these precautions, four years later one new puppy, Dancer, was poisoned. Three other dogs living in our own neighborhood block also died from poison. Area residents knew the source.

How could any human who owned her own dog have such little regard for the lives and suffering of other people's loving, loyal, and innocent animals? Had she no conscience? Someday, I would change the world… for animals.

In but a few months, Christmas morning, 1952, a family tragedy would change the way our family spent our time and our lives. I would need that time, time I had previously devoted to searching and caring for abandoned pets, so that I could assume some very serious responsibilities in family matters. Mother, only forty years old, suffered a blood clot, necessitating that her trusted and skilled surgeons amputate her left hand.

In each of the previous seven years, she had been hospitalized in a large health facility built in 1926 for railroad employees, AT&SF Railroad Memorial Hospital in Albuquerque, 240 miles to the west. Surgery had been necessary, on each prior occasion, to remove a blood clot in one of her limbs. During her 1951 visit, her physicians, rather than to once again surgically remove a clot in her left arm, opted to prescribe a newly introduced anti-coagulant trial medication, Coumadin, which was used as a blood thinner to treat thromboembolism, the formation and movement of blood clots in blood vessels. However, it would not be approved for medical use until 1954.

While under its treatment, she remained on hospital grounds for six weeks for observation. The last week in February, her prognosis was good. We were elated. Her physicians reported that this drug had caused the clot to slowly dissolve; the blood supply to her left arm had returned. She was released and returned to work in Riley's Switch. Because Memorial hospital staff was under the impression that the clot had completely dissolved, no order was issued for her local physician in Riley's Switch to monitor her situation. Nine months later, they learned that the effect of Coumadin had not been total. A small portion of the clot had remained, growing, until, on December 25, Christmas morning, 1952, it completely blocked her artery in her left arm.

Our hospital in Riley's Switch was not always in a stage of accreditation, so Mother (suffering silently in the unimaginable pain associated with gangrene), Delia and I boarded the train that evening for Albuquerque, only one hour, a long hour, after Mother's emergency began. All compartments and seats on coach and Pullman were taken, so we rode in the train's spacious ladies' room.

Her stay in AT&SF RR Memorial Hospital in Albuquerque required the medical expertise of various specialists, hospital personnel and entailed several operations. She remained an in-patient for a lengthy and agonizing four and a half months. It would be necessary that ChooDaddy remain at home to tend to the needs of Aunt Martha and Sandy. To visit our alone and frightened mother mandated that Delia and I take compartments or overnight sleepers on AT&SF RR, every weekend, using railroad passes, complimentary for family members of railroad employees. This was a frightening and uneasy period of major upheaval and stress for our family. Mother urged us to "pray faster."

While we were traveling, kind and concerned conductors kept a watchful eye on the superintendent's granddaughters. Sometimes we were fortunate to be accompanied by Mucio Yslas, a protective friend and treasured employee of both ChooDaddy and AT&SF. Once we arrived, we were met by employee-friends of ChooDaddy's. We had standing weekend reservations in the Alvarado Hotel, located on railroad property, less than ten blocks, an easy walk, to the hospital.

The three of us, Delia, Mother and I, had birthdays during the three weeks preceding Valentine's Day. I pondered on a special way for us to still celebrate our birthdays together, even in the bleak hospital setting. Without the expert help of the adults in our household, I spent hours baking for Mother a homemade, heart-shaped, reddish cake. I was disappointed that after adding one, then two, and finally three bottles of liquid red food coloring to my cake batter, it still remained an unappetizing rust color, and, after baked, it seemed rather heavy. "It's the thought that counts," I calmly repeated.

My icing didn't quite turn out like the recipe picture either. But finding the perfect-sized cake box and some heart-shaped doilies from a nearby bakery lifted my spirits. I was prepared for our important weekend trip.

When I proudly presented my Valentine-birthday cake to Mother at the hospital (she had tubes and monitors attached to almost every part of her small frame), her eyes lit up. With difficulty, she smiled and asked her nurse to please cut it for us and include the staff in the celebration.

I noticed that it seemed very difficult to slice, but I thought it might be due to a dull hospital knife. "I should have brought a sharp knife from home," I apologized.

That overcooked, doughy and dense cake, with its grainy and concrete-like icing provided our family (and the hospital staff, I am sure) with a multitude of jokes for years, but I was pleased that it made my mother's birthday a happier one—and after all, that was my intention.

During the next twenty years, my mother's health would require about ten more emergency visits to Memorial Hospital, with stays lasting from two to thirteen weeks. Our family often discussed that without the AT&SF RR medical plan, based on employee and employer contributions, the thirty years in which my mother's health required constant surgical, medical and hospital care would have surely bankrupted our family.

Although Mother returned home in May 1953 with a new prosthesis to replace her lost limb, she also had to return again, nine years after her first classes in 1943, to Benson Business School, to relearn the skill of typing, but this time, with only one hand. Her speed, two months later, was remarkable, exceeding 100 words per minute. When Mother, as a child, was recovering from polio in her right leg, she was taught by her wise mother to consider the word "can't" as a challenge, and she did.

We were so proud of her typing scores. Certainly no one anticipated the welcome she would receive from her boss at AT&SF, Caird Donatell. "Eileen, your amputation has made you unfit for your job. We do not hire the handicapped."

After calls from ChooDaddy to Chicago Headquarters of AT&SF, he spoke with several of his fellow administrators. The following day, Mother began a new position at AT&SF with a more decent supervisor. A hardworking and knowledgeable employee, she would not retire for twenty-one more years.

At home, this fiercely independent lady devised several shortcuts to help her overcome performing daily tasks, once considered mundane but now difficult, with the use of only one hand. These included two patented inventions. The first was a machete-shaped knife for cutting meat, a tool now used by disabled veterans. During my daily cooking routines, I am reminded of her second idea, which she sold to Betty Crocker. Because of her innovative mind, the wrappings of oleo, margarine and butter are marked with measurements of teaspoons, tablespoons and cups. This is but one example why her bravery and strength were spoken of and admired by the hospital staffs, her neighbors, friends, office associates and, basically by most who were fortunate enough to meet her.

During 1957, the second semester of my freshman year at University of New Mexico (UNM), in Albuquerque, 240 miles away from Riley's Switch, Mother called for me to come home immediately. ChooDaddy had been hospitalized with pneumonia, and his prognosis was poor. This great man (*Who's Who in American Railroads, Who's Who in New Mexico*) had been responsible for a multitude of untold kind acts throughout his eighty-six years.

Our community was deeply indebted to him for his generosity and kindness. For those two months when the school system had lacked sufficient funds to pay their teachers, ChooDaddy wrote a check to make up the difference. During the three years in the 1930's that our town had exorbitant unemployment, ChooDaddy had Sunday dinners in our yard, redwood picnic tables overflowing with food for families whose parents who could not find work. "You can't properly search for work on an empty stomach," was his reasoning.

He was my teacher, my champion, my rock. He had mastered the power of giving and of quiet acceptance. I wanted to emulate his example when I became an adult woman.

We were able to speak for but a short time before he died. As I held his frail hand during those hours, with difficulty, he spoke, "Kate, I am very proud of you."

"ChooDaddy, how can you possibly be proud of me? I haven't done anything."

"My being proud of you is because of who you have become. What you do is reflective of that person."

Without ChooDaddy, we all were lost, but his beloved Sandy more so, as she refused to eat, even when we warmed her food, like ChooDaddy did, "to boost its aroma." In vain, we tried every treat, every tasty morsel that we thought she might enjoy. Our veterinarian explained that sometimes dogs simply die of heartbreak when they have lost their beloved owners. And she did.

Scamp was guardian of our hearts, but not of our home.

CHAPTER 6

BRAVEHEART

"Saving just one dog won't change the world, but surely it will change the world...for that one dog."
— **Fur and Feather Animal Assistance Inc.**

That May, between my freshman and sophomore year at UNM, I landed, what I thought was a glamorous summer job, waitress at an internationally recognized resort at Santa Fe's Bishop's Lodge, nestled in 450 acres of national forest lands of the Sangre de Cristo Mountains. Because it was but a few miles from the home of our hospitable cousins, Charles and Bethie White in Teseque, NM, it made it very convenient for Mother and my sister, Delia, to come from Riley's Switch for weekend visits. Mother's mother (my Farley-Smyer grandmother) and Charles' mother were close sisters. Both married and lived in New Mexico, and their children, about the same ages, had strong, loyal friendships.

During the last week in July, we agreed that a dog could help the loneliness we felt with the February deaths of ChooDaddy and his Sandy. We anticipated that it would possibly take several visits in the next few months to Santa Fe Animal Shelter and Humane Society (Riley's Switch did not have a shelter) before we could find the right dog for our home. But on our first visit, just as we entered the shelter door, a woman was surrendering "our to-be dog." Her concerned daughter had discovered him wandering behind their convenience store in the foothills.

Varying shades and patterns of long golden-brown, wavy hair adorned this handsome Cocker Spaniel-Beagle cross puppy. He wagged his long, beautiful tail non-stop., sweeping up all the pet hair on the shelter's linoleum floor. His large brown eyes, outlined by a large golden-haired mask, were mesmerizing. He "had us" at our first glance into those pleading eyes. Because of his resemblance to the dog in the Disney movie, *Lady and The Tramp*, we named him Scamp.

Although he was in constant motion, Scamp was surprisingly easy to train. For a very short time, we even entertained the thought that he might also be a watchdog for the three single women at home. Anytime Scamp heard our doorbell, just like most dogs, he howled. But if our visitor happened to be a male (any age), he would tuck tail and scamper silently and quickly under or behind the flowered living-room couch. Delia and I snickered and nickname him "Mother's BraveHeart."

Was this a behavioral quirk or a result of his life before we found him?

Scamp's face wrinkled to register his disappointment that Delia would actually entertain her steady boyfriend, a male, in our living room, causing an automatic retreat by her frightened pooch. By choice he remained in the kitchen with Mother and me while Delia and Ray giggled, whispered and behaved like the teenagers they were.

What wonderful adventures we shared with Scamp during the years! Our summer trips to Red River cabins were a mountainous adventure with hours of hiking and fishing. Our weekend backyard picnics meant a shared feast for Scamper. But his favorite always seemed to be our outings at nearby Oasis State Park, located eighteen miles southwest of Riley's Switch. Though small, it was refreshing to play around a lake, and a welcome relief from the flat, dry, barren, grasslands of Riley's Switch. We would sit, with our girlfriend guests, on one of the many stones or boulders outlining the small lake, and share ChooDaddy's bulky and almost ancient binoculars, with scratched lenses and a broken leather strap.

Home to an assortment of interesting and colorful

birds in its surrounding tall cottonwood trees, we spotted jays, flickers, flycatchers, finches, doves—and sparrows, of course. Occasionally we would spy a red-tailed hawk, an eagle or even a nocturnal owl. Quail and pheasants were common. But the prized sighting was always our comical New Mexico state bird, the roadrunner, as it darted between native shrubs. A member of the cuckoo family, this avian predator can reach speeds up to 15 m.p.h.

Whatever new skill-testing physical feats and games we contrived while jumping from boulder to boulder at Oasis, Scamp would follow, gleefully running, splashing and swimming in the pond. After all, he was a Spaniel. But he lacked the hunting traits associated with his breed. Scamp never chased after any animal, at home or during any of our family travels.

My favorite trips were our week-long summer vacations to Red River, a heavily wooded resort town, altitude 8,750 feet, in the Sangre de Cristo Mountains in northern New Mexico about thirty-nine miles south of Colorado. Our three-bedroom rustic cabin was located at scenic Hickman's Ranch, a family-owned and-managed resort, on which their approximately fifty log cabins were built around two man-made private lakes, stocked daily with rainbow, brook and cutthroat trout.

Although pets were not allowed, Mr. Hickman made an exception for Scamp, whose good behavior and quiet manner earned him to be worthy of this privilege, as long as, when outdoors, he remained on-leash. We would sit by the lake, cast our line, loaded with approved fireballs, (no slimy wiggly worms for us) and enjoy a good read in the shade of the many pines and firs beautifying this unique property.

Hickman's Ranch was a wonderful vacation for all.
PHOTO BY JOE ZELLER

Scamp, on-leash, was happy to snooze beside us. Seldom did we "catch" dinner, but fresh trout was available for sale at Hickman's Market, situated next to their office on one of the lakes.

Our cleaning and deboning processes brought exaggerated grimaces and cries of disgust. The actual dipping of them in a fresh batter of cornmeal and frying them set culinary standards back several years by reinventing the number of ways young girls can interpret or change a simple recipe. Although we always prepared a filet for Scamp, our creative cooking skills sometimes resulted in his food dish being filled with several leftover portions of greasy and over-cooked "blackened" trout.

I always looked forward to playing with Scamp when I would return home from Albuquerque, either as a student at the University of New Mexico, or as a secondary teacher for Albuquerque Public Schools. No pets were allowed in UNM's Kappa Kappa Gamma sorority house or in the apartments I rented while teaching. When visiting at home during my next six years of school holidays, Scamp provided a much-needed but temporary "dog fix." He was the beloved companion and quiet confidant of the whole family.

Delia and I tried unsuccessfully many evenings to tempt him with an assortment of his favorite treats so that he would sleep in one of our bedrooms. Yet Scamp always chose to sleep with Mother. We kidded ourselves that it was because she was an early riser, thus assuring him of an early breakfast. The truth was that his devotion for her outweighed our paltry treat-temptations. Scamp loyally trailed after and dogged Mother's heels everywhere when she was home.

During his last six years, Mother had retired as a clerk from the AT&SF RR and once again began rescuing stray, abandoned dogs. The neighborhood threat of poisoning was no more. Her homeless critters not only provided canine company for Scamp but also necessitated that he hasten his gait to keep up with some of the younger pups. Scamp had a rich, very long and full life, eighteen years, until, in July, 1975, when my loving, courageous, proud and resourceful Mother died, soon after which her "BraveHeart" joined her in the heavens. Maybe God is a woman.

Our Mr. Mullins was loved, but lost.

CHAPTER 7

THE WRONG CHOICE

"Though but a dog, he readily accepts my frailties, understanding that I am but a human."

– C.E. Smyer

In 1962, during my third year of teaching middle-school in Albuquerque, I met and married my honey-heart, Wally, a dentist from New Jersey who was stationed at Cannon Air Force Base near Riley's Switch. With his intrinsically honest, kind and generous manner, he reminded me of my beloved ChooDaddy. Before we married, we spoke of a shared commitment, using our limited resources and efforts, to change for the better the way pets were perceived, and therefore, treated. We agreed that Wally would take the New Mexico Dental Board so that we could continue to reside in the state, because we both appreciated its open spaces, magnificent vistas, painted sunsets, diverse cultures, and a laid-back style of life.

All states then required that any dentist who practiced in their state must pass their individual state board, a practical and written exam scheduled at varying times, usually annually. Because of the aftermath of the Cuban Missile Crisis, Wally was still on alert at Cannon, a Tactical Air Command Air Force base, when the New Mexico State Dental Boards were given in July 1963 at the state penitentiary. That emergency military alert dictated that he remain a few miles of Riley's Switch, meaning he would be unable to travel 215 miles to Santa Fe for the dental exam. Without that New Mexico license, we would not be able to remain in my home state.

We were fortunate that upon graduating from Temple Dental School in Philadelphia, Pennsylvania, in 1961, Wally had already passed the New Jersey State Board Dental Examination and was licensed to practice there. So we had no choice. In August 1963, his discharge date from the service, we left our friends and my family in Riley's

Switch and moved to his home, southern New Jersey. We both labored hard and pinched pennies to earn the calculated funds to return to New Mexico for the June Dental Boards in 1965.

Wally practiced dentistry in Vineland and Beverly, spending many harried hours on the New Jersey Turnpike and state roads daily, driving between the two offices and our new home, Buttonwood Courts Garden Apartments in Maple Shade. This was his exhausting routine as he traveled in our faded blue 1960 Volkswagen more than 150 miles daily, six days a week, from early morning into the late evening hours.

I was teaching at Cherry Hill High School (CHHS), a sizeable and first rate learning institution located in an upscale, cosmopolitan community near our Maple Shade apartment. I was pleasantly surprised with the outstanding quality of the New Jersey school system. Excellence was reflected in their teachers, administration and curriculums. They were accountable, impressive and progressive, far ahead of ours in New Mexico. It truly opened my eyes to the caliber of education that was available to students in other states. Their current graduation rate is 99.7 and their percentage of students eligible for free or reduced-cost lunches was only 6.2. In Albuquerque Public Schools, our graduation rate barely exceeds 63 percent and nearly one-third of our students receive free or reduced lunch benefits.

Another surprise came when it was obvious that, regardless of their outstanding schools, most New Jersey residents, including teachers, were under the false impression that New Mexico had not yet experienced statehood.

They were curious but uninformed, as reflected by their bizarre questions.

"Do you have safeguards against bacteria in your food and water?"

"How is your mail delivered?"

"Is there a customs duty or a tax on your letters and packages?"

"Are many of your roads paved?"

"Do many residents ride horses to work?"

"Is English your second language?"

Thousands of other New Mexicans experienced these questions and for the last twenty years have submitted them to be shared in the column, "One of Our Fifty Is Missing" in the *New Mexico Magazine*.

Because we were a one-car couple, I depended on other teachers living nearby for rides to and from CHHS. By four o'clock on most afternoons, I returned to our empty nest, knowing no one in the apartment complex. I felt sure that the perfect solution to my loneliness would be a dog. (Where have you heard that before?) Our Buttonwood Court resident-manager listened to our request, and then recited the apartment rules forbidding pets.

Not long after we were refused a pet, Wally and I were walking about the complex and noticed a perplexing site. A young blonde woman was rhythmically disappearing up and down in her window. Our curiosity got the best of us. Rudely, we peeked into her window and discovered that she was just riding an exercise bicycle. We also discovered that in a handlebar basket on that bicycle sat a darling apricot Teacup Poodle. *No dogs?*

When we confronted the manager with this newly

*Mr. Mullins and buddy, Happy Hill, enjoyed play sessions
in apartment's grassed courtyard.*

obtained information, he discounted it because she was
the "friend" of the apartment owner and therefore exempt.
I did not see it quite that way and waited until the owner,
whom we had previously met, paid a visit to his "friend." I
presented our case, explaining that we too wanted to enjoy
the many pleasures of having a dog. What a surprise! His
"friend" interceded, and their slightly bent pet rule was sus-
pended for us also.

No surprise…we got a dog, a handsome, playful Beagle puppy from Collingswood, a nearby town. Wally and
I named him Mr. Mullins, appropriate because the color
configuration of his coat resembled that of an English but-
ler. My younger readings had exposed me to the English
family crest of the Mullins family.

For the remaining year and a half in New Jersey, I left
my clothes for him to sleep on, so my scent would keep him
company while I was teaching. He greeted me eagerly with

a happy bark and a wagging tail each day when I returned from school. For the long five hours until Wally would return from work, we would walk, read, talk, play and delight in each other's company. Because he was so aware and well behaved, Wally and I could and did take him everywhere that allowed dogs. He was never destructive or disruptive. New neighbors from Texas moved upstairs and with them, their darling beagle, Happy Hill.

In July 1965 Wally and I traveled back to New Mexico, where for three grueling days he took the State Dental Board, held in the Penitentiary of New Mexico basement in Santa Fe, the colorful state capital, often referred to as "The City Different" and one of the most tourist frequented cities in the southwest. Founded in 1610, it is a center of multi-cultural arts reflective of our state's diverse demographics.

The New Mexico exam was notoriously political, as were most state boards, of "so-called vacation states," passing and granting licenses mostly to home-grown applicants. Goose-necked lamps proved poor light while prison patients sat in wooden, straight-backed chairs and guards reminded attending dentists to be cautious with their sharp instruments. Spending these stressful days with Wally were other applicants, some of whom, despite having passed other state boards, were re-taking the New Mexico state exam.

None of the dental examiners were aware of Wally's ties to two old New Mexico families (one before 1912 statehood). Although his scores were in the higher ninety-percentile, his name was not to be included in the list of those accepted. How fortunate we were that, quite by accident, my Riley's Switch Uncle Clem, now from Colorado, was visiting in Santa Fe and encountered his adopted brother, one of the dental board examiners! Because Uncle Clem inquired about Wally's progress on the dental exams and mentioned his in-laws, Wally's name appeared on the "passed" list. Thank goodness! Prayers, via Uncle Clem, were answered. How eerie that this particular uncle would be the individual instrumental in Wally's passing the board and our desired return to New Mexico!

Wally had been under considerable pressure during our past two years in New Jersey with his endless traveling between offices. Add to that stress the fact that I was unhappy, not adjusting well to New Jersey life, the humidity, dense population, and harsh winters. His passing the New Mexico Dental Board exam was great cause for celebration. Little did we know that our life in New Mexico would be filled with those special blessings that animal rescue can bring.

In August 1965 we said our goodbyes to our friends and Wally's family and drove our new blue Chevrolet Impala almost 2,000 miles to Albuquerque, the largest city in New Mexico. At that time, its population was only 193,000. Its subsequent surge of growth is evidenced by the current population tally exceeding 550,000 residents. Albuquerque's panoramic view is bound by two mountain ranges, the Sandia and Manzano, on the east, and two Indian pueblos, Sandia and Isleta, on the north, Kirtland Air Force Base on the south, and the ancient rock-art petroglyphs inscribed near inert volcanoes on the west. A river, the Rio Grande, runs through its valleys and farms on the west. Its climate is mild, sunny and dry; its elevation ranges from 4,900 to 6,700 feet.

Mr. Mullins gave us a "heady" welcome home.

Wally entered private practice with another dentist (recommended by a supposed friend), who kept him on emergency call for seven evenings a week and all day during weekends. It seemed as if Wally was called out on an "emergency" during every University of New Mexico Lobo game that we attended. Although it was definitely a strain, Wally patiently persevered, and within five years, by 1970, he had his own practice. Another cause for celebration!

My present teaching assignment was Rio Grande High School, fifteen miles to the southwest of our apartment. Mr. Mullins remained my eager afternoon greeter, sticking his handsome head and long ears under our second-story apartment balcony railing and howling a "Hello." I felt fortunate to have such a loving dog place his head on my lap as I graded my class papers in the evenings.

We brought home a darling Pug puppy that year, Beulah. They quickly bonded and provided companionship for one another while we were away at work.

My sister, Delia, a very easy house-guest, had moved into our apartment with us and was employed by a local accounting firm. Albuquerque was close enough, 240 miles, for Mother to board the train from Riley's Switch for visits. We were all working toward an obtainable goal and making progress. Life was good.

Yet Wally and I were to be blessed to enjoy our perky, bright Mr. Mullins for only five years. After the birth of our first child, Miss Kate in 1967, we were shocked when Mr. Mullins repeatedly tried to attack her. Realizing that Mr. Mullins and Beulah would be deprived of the endless human attention they previously enjoyed "before-baby," Wally and I had made sure that we continued to include them in everything. We still took both for their usual car rides, baked their special chicken treats, and played games with them. They still were enjoying the petting and fussing over him while they rested each evening, on the same pillow at the foot of our bed.

But this new baby girl was now taking much of our time, time we had previously devoted to spoiling our two canines. And while Beulah accepted her birth with a "ho-hum," Mr. Mullins was not to be placated. Many visits to several veterinarians and pet behavioralists resulted in only a minor lessening of his unhappiness and aggression. Although there were no more attacks or "growlings," he continued to lift on the legs of her baby bed, chew on her little toys and defecate on her blankets and linens.

Although Beulah seemed perfectly content with Miss Kate, her attitude did not influence or change the unacceptable behavior of Mr. Mullins. It was now 1969, and we had been trying to change Mr. Mullins's behavior without success for two years. Nothing seemed to completely alleviate this potential dangerous situation. Miss Kate was now almost two years old, and a new baby boy was due in a few months. We were forced to confront the fact that we had made the wrong decision in getting Mr. Mullins before we had our first child. Feeling such sorrow, we knew that we were left with no other choice but to find for our wonderful and loving Mr. Mullins another good home, without children. What a terrible sense of loneliness, abandonment and confusion he must have felt!

I felt as if our surrendering him was my fault, due to my selfishness, needing a dog before we had our first child. Some couples accomplish this feat easily, but our attempt was a mistake, a bad choice, that ended tragically. While I was having great difficulty adjusting to New Jersey, its different attitudes, customs and weather, my Mr. Mullins brightened my unhappy and lonely days. Yet now I had just betrayed him and broken his heart. His very special place in my heart has never been filled.

Miss Kate and Beulah wait for Santa, 1967.

CHAPTER 8

BEULAH THE BOSS

"Pugs possess a sense of entitlement termed pug-tude that is unrelentless."

While still living in southern New Jersey, I was reconnoitering one Saturday in the nearby, famous and humongous Cherry Hill Mall while Wally was busy working in the dental clinic at Vineland State School and Hospital. I was drawn, of course, to their pet emporium. Inside, there were many different purebreds represented as well as an assortment of mixed breeds. In one kennel, I found a comical-featured dog whose appearance I would visualize as a Bulldog-cross with bat-like ears and the nose of a pig. I had never before seen a dog like this, and whatever the combinations, this mixed-breed puppy in the cage was absolutely adorable. It was flat-faced with large, protruding dark eyes. Its small and sturdy barrel-like frame sported thick and deeply wrinkled fur. The tightly multi-curled tail was like the "cherry on the top." If this had been my puppy, I would have named her "Uh-Oh." As not to poke too much fun at this unforgettable puppy with a large, round head, I smilingly referred to it as "of unknown ancestry."

The haughty but well-informed sales lady was quick to correct my ignorance, which she found offensive, and informed me of a Pug's thoroughbred and attributes. "Your assessment is completely incorrect. A Pug is certainly not a mixed breed and certainly not a miniature Bulldog. Haven't you seen their pictures as the chosen pets of the Duke and Duchess of Windsor? The Pug, an AKC-classified toy dog, is originally from China, dating back before the 16th century. The breed motto is '*multum in parvo*,' a lot in a small package. They are prized for their total devotion to their master."

Where in the genetic gene pool of a Pug could you find hidden the DNA of the wolf, ancestor of all dogs?

I was still broadly smiling as I exited the pet store, thinking that this sixteen pound, bright-eyed, curly-tailed breed would make a perfect companion and foil to our exceedingly handsome and distinguished Mr. Mullins.

Not until we returned to New Mexico in 1965 did we purchase, at a "three-hour sale," this canine choice of the Duke and Duchess of Windsor. We named our new Pug puppy, fawn with black mask, Beulah. Extremely easy to train, this affectionate, patient but determined dog fit right into our family and immediately became a constant little companion and cuddling chum of our darling Mr. Mullins, who had never met a dog or cat he didn't like. But welcoming our new baby girl into the family was not on his agenda.

Like most dogs, our new Pug was wary of anything with wheels. In 1968 her senses were forced into "fine-tune" when we purchased for Miss Kate a baby-walker. (What a misnomer!). Our small and dainty little girl became a whirling dervish, gleefully racing with abandonment within the confines of our family room. Once those multi-directional wheels began to roll, Beulah would, like a flash, jump onto the hearth of the fireplace and become perfectly still, barely breathing. The only thing that moved was her eyes. She blended into its cream stonework (protective coloration), unnoticed, until our daughter rolled past her.

When not in a traveling mode, Miss Kate enjoyed pretending to read some small cloth children's book, usually held upside down, to a long-suffering Beulah, whom she affectionately called "Boo." A wonderful companion for Miss Kate, Beulah seemed immune to pats instead of pets and to Miss Kate's constant curiosity with that tightly wrapped curly tail.

By June 1969 Beulah had another small child to contend with, our newly born son, Kurt, whom at first she totally ignored. He mostly slept. There were so many other humans in Beulah's household who were awake and in need of her verbal directions, so she thought. She even carried her bossiness to Riley's Switch. Because of her small, compact size and usually quiet disposition, Beulah was easy to take on car trips to visit my mother who still lived in Riley's Switch. Scamp (aka BraveHeart) still dogged Mother's heels. But when Mother was not in the house, Scamp, tail wagging, would happily follow dictatorial Beulah The Boss everywhere… unless it was to a room where Wally (a male) was present. "Follow the Leader" only goes so far, and Scamp remained steadfast in his distrust of men.

Beulah's bark meant business. Stubborn, sturdy and vocal, Beulah not only bossed and corralled all members of our young and growing family but also "mothered" several rescue dogs that needed tenderness and guidance.

One such dog was Tangles, who jumped over our six-foot cinderblock wall, into our back yard one morning and ran to the corner, shivering and howling unceasingly. He appeared to be a Miniature Poodle-cross, with a long, curly, dark and tangled coat. Visits with our veterinarian and groomer revealed that he was a grossly underweight puppy (twelve pounds), had impaired vision, and was, to our surprise, white. Tangles was very smart and exceptionally agile and quick, much to the chagrin of the sedentary Beulah. He never shed, which is the complete opposite of Pugs, who leave behind a thick cloud of hair, flowing through the air and onto the floor, in every room they visit.

Another ward that Beulah "nannied" was a lively black

Pearly wants to play.

Pug puppy, Pearly, who enjoyed playing hide-and-seek in the dark, narrow space under our king-sized bed. Our arm spans were not that long, making her impossible to reach, although our accumulation of dust bunnies certainly came out in abundance. But when we would pretend to give up her game, she would dash to us as we were supposedly leaving the room, bark, wag her curly black tail, and run back towards the bed—her challenge for us to try again and again and again.

Just like Beulah, Pearly shed a lot, but she was a great family dog: clean, calm and fun-loving. But before she could even reach her first birthday, she swallowed a sandwich laced with a poison and thrown over our back wall. It happened so suddenly that I barely saw the boy's face as he purposefully tossed it into our yard and ran across the street to the nearby high school.

We tried to explain and ease Pearly's sudden death to

Miss Kate by describing a picture of Pearly in Heaven, hiding under and pouncing from cloud to cloud. A few days later, a single black hair was evident in my morning dust pan, and my tears flowed. The roles were switched. My four-year-old daughter tried to console her grieving mother. "You said Pearly was in Heaven with baby Jesus, but, Mother, won't she leave her black hair all over His white robes when she jumps on His lap?"

In 1976, when Beulah was ten, we moved into a new neighborhood. Within only a few years, she fell victim to both arthritis and glaucoma, and was bent. She was blind in one eye. Her hearing was impaired. The steps to her new back yard were becoming more difficult by the day. Her health continued to fail. Our veterinarian diagnosed kidney failure when she became incontinent.

"Is Beulah in pain? She still has a good appetite and wags her tail. Would it be selfish for us to put her in diapers and tend to her until she is in discomfort?" With heavy hearts, we voiced these concerns to the vet.

He cautioned us that once we noticed a major weight loss or disorientation, we should show her the respect that she had earned and schedule her final appointment with him. In only five short weeks, the signs were there. She was becoming painfully thin. The appointment was set, two days away. The following morning went according to routine. After feeding Beulah, I opened the door so she could relieve herself in the yard. Within an hour, I was searching that fenced-in yard, in vain, for Beulah. She was not to be found.

Did Beulah sense what was going to happen? How did this elderly and sick dog get out of our fenced-in property?

Quickly Miss Kate and Kurt joined the search. We

frantically searched our entire acre and three-quarters, but no Beulah. Three concerned neighbors helped us as we continued our search throughout the neighborhood for hours. Evening had set in and no sign of our Beulah. She was small, elderly, partially blind and deaf—helpless, without defenses. Traffic on our street speeded unchecked. Nearby coyotes could be heard howling at night. I do not fare well in that type of situation, and I was almost hysterical. I had worked myself into a worrying frenzy and spent a sleepless night. The next morning we sent out alarms to City Animal Services and Animal Humane Services, and prayed and searched.

At noon I received a puzzling call from a resident of our neighborhood who operated a cabinetry business several miles away. He had, by accident, discovered Beulah that morning, resting in the middle of his residential street, a considerable distance from our home.

There was no mistaking the controlled anger in his voice. "My wife and I are appalled. This little old dog's paws were bloody. She is so thin that we can see her ribs. We are concerned that you might have abused her. We got your phone number from her tags, but are considering not returning her to you. I just wanted you to know that we have contacted the City Animal Services."

What a shocker! Thank goodness she was alive!

"Thank you for calling and for your kindness. Our family has been up all night, searching all through the neighborhood for her. We were worried sick. Our dog's name is Beulah. My family loves her deeply and cares for her responsibly. But she is old and has serious medical problems: failing kidneys, arthritis, and glaucoma. Her paw pads are bloody, because she somehow got out of our fenced-in yard and walked the two miles to your home. Thank you for finding her. Thank you for calling us.

"Please call our veterinarian, Dr. McKenna, about her health and inquire about the care she receives from us. She has never been abused, just spoiled, but I want you to hear that from her vet. After you have spoken with him, would you please call me back, so we can arrange to pick her up at your place of business?"

The minute I hung up the phone, I sobbed with relief that she had been found. I was greatly saddened for her new injuries and upset by the awful, unfounded accusations.

When I contacted Wally at his office, we were both dumbfounded that her little crippled legs could have carried her that far. I picked up our stubborn Beulah, paws wrapped, from the distrusting but kind neighbor at his woodworking shop. He and his wife, although they had spoken with our veterinarian, were still wary of releasing her to me. Within minutes, she was with our vet, having her paws examined, medicated and re-wrapped. I also cancelled her final appointment. It would be rescheduled when she was not so determined to live, which was months in the future. The Boss would let us know, and she did, without an appointment.

Dana endures a Kurt and Miss Kate hug, 1976.

CHAPTER 9

OUR GREAT ONE

"If dogs don't go to heaven, then when I die I want to go where the dogs are."

– Will Rogers

Our new and larger home had considerable land, almost two wooded acres, in the foothills of the Manzano Mountains. Because of the abundance of wildlife, some dangerous, we would have to keep a closer watch on our dogs when they were outside in our large, fenced-in yard. Over the years we would be visited by a multitude of wildlilfe scents: deer, raccoon, skunks, squirrels, coyotes, chipmunks, roadrunners, snakes and even feral cats and bobcats.

There would be three occasions of which we were aware when our fruiting apple trees lured unwanted, hungry Black Bears over our six-foot fence and into the side yard for an easy snack. The last sighting in 2011 by observant neighbors brought New Mexico Department of Game and Fish (NMDGF) leaping over our fences and into our yard, for several scary and unannounced visits.

Bears are often forced from our nearby mountains, both the Manzanos and Sandias, when intense drought conditions or winter hard freezes result in lack of natural foods. Once they become habituated to human surroundings, these bears are a danger, and must be captured and relocated between thirty to fifty miles away by state game officers. That is not considered to be a big distance for the Black Bears, New Mexico's official animal. A return visit can be cause for this highly intelligent, vulnerable mammal to be euthanized. In 2011 NMDGF received more than 115 bear complaints in the Sandias. In comparison to the thirty-two in 2009, this became a critical issue for our state's wildlife management.

In September 2012 we were surprised by a photo collection, taken that month and shared by a neighbor two homes away, of a smallish mountain lion roaming in her back yard and also in her neighbor's to the east. What a shock we had when she showed us one snapshot showing the puma standing by our own wrought-iron gate! These incidents, along with the bears and the coyotes, alerted and frightened the pet owners in these limited blocks into becoming much more alert and observant.

We formed a loosely organized neighborhood watch for wildlife. Sightings of coyotes were much more frequent, and the cause of warning phone calls between neighbors almost monthly, as they had been responsible for the demise of a few pets in our neighborhood. Those of us who chose to live in these outlying areas were fortunate to experience, first-hand, New Mexico's wildlife, but we also were forced to adjust to that existing wildlife, all of which were beautiful, some of which were dangerous.

However, my state in 2012 and 2013, demonstrated its insensitivity to the Circle-of-Life concept and the precarious balance of nature. It showed its blatant ignorance of wildlife conservation and sound land management. No population explosions of coyotes and no increased livestock killings by this canine predator prompted this action. It was simply an activity to provide fun for ego-pumped hunters who have no conscience. The New Mexico state game commissioner actually sanctioned contests for the indiscriminate, cruel, mass killings of coyotes. The sponsors touted, "Any method—the more the better." slogans. Prizes offered by Los Lunas and Roswell gun shops were a choice of a shotgun or semi-automatic rifles.

"These hunts are just a great way to have some fun … and a chance to win some great prizes," was the widely printed opinion of our state game commissioner. Such hunts are scheduled in several New Mexico gun-toting communities where ranchers bemoan the foul deeds of coyotes. Under scrutiny, statistics from the U.S. Department of Agriculture reveal a different story, as less than three percent of livestock kills can be attributed to coyotes.

A 2013 house bill that would ban coyote hunts was shunned by our legislators, who voted mainly by political party and killed Bill 316. Since they went against the wishes of thousands of e-mail signatures of New Mexico voters who had urged its passage, to whom were our legislators listening?

Returning to 1976, our new home had ample room not just for an assortment of wildlife, but also for a Great Dane puppy. This regal beauty was a fortieth birthday surprise for Wally. "But all I wanted was a necktie," he quipped. His eyes were wide with shock as he tried to absorb the size of his ten-week old, fifty-pound beauty queen, still sporting pink curlers in her recently cropped ears until their cartilage hardened.

"Dad, I've named her Dana. What else could we possibly name a girl Great Dane?" our excited daughter, Miss Kate, asked. "Mother wanted to call her Trigger." For the first few weeks our son, Kurt, was so enamored with her that he would drag his sleeping bag into the family room and sleep next to her.

In spite of her size she was surprisingly gentle, quiet and agile. When one of our friends visited with her small, three-year-old son, our Dana's reaction was a surprise. She dropped to the floor, moving forward only on her front elbows and back haunches, thus greatly minimizing her size and not frightening our tiny guest. It worked like a charm. This exploring toddler was not intimidated by Dana and spent the morning crawling on and over Dana, the picture of patience.

Within just a few years, our Dana had grown into a statuesque, 160-pound dog and presented an imposing creature to our friends. Most of them reacted by shaking their heads in shock and disbelief. They were in total agreement that this time we had lost complete control of our faculties.

Because of Dana's size, markings, gait and other official standards for Great Danes, her breeder implored us to let him train her for American Kennel Club (AKC) confirmation. But we were already aware that Dana's sensitivity caused negative reactions, physically, to loud noises or the slightest change of tone. New environments caused gastric upsets. More important, Wally and I disagreed with AKC policy that spayed or neutered dogs were not eligible to compete in confirmation events, because these shows and competitions are intended to evaluate breeding stock. Throughout our years of rescue work, we had encountered a heartbreaking number of throw-aways, many of which were purebreds, some AKC registered with paperwork. Wally and I agreed that all of our dogs, regardless of ancestry, would be spayed or neutered, a responsible measure.

Due to her sheer size and her super-sensitivity, Dana added a different dimension to our family life. Until obedience classes were completed, she drag-walked us. Until obedience classes were completed, her deafening bark drowned the ringing of the telephone or doorbell. And until obedience classes were completed, all clothing left in the family room was consumed as a special treat, excepting the soles to Kurt's tennis shoes, moistened but not eaten.

On her first Easter, much to the kids' chagrin, Dana naturally assumed the lead role when the time came to hunt for colored eggs. In record time, our carefully hidden eggs for our family had been discovered, broken, slobbered upon, and no longer were desirable to Miss Kate or Kurt. So we learned to hold an earlier egg-hunt for Dana and Beulah with eggs dyed just for them.

Dana posed a much larger responsibility for Beulah, who was in denial that she had long since relinquished her alpha-role. She tagged along with Dana everywhere, acting as "mentor." They were almost inseparable, a bizarre coupling, particularly when Beulah slept curled up inside Dana's long awkward legs. What a comical pair they presented! Our Beulah, our Boss, finally relinquished her ruling spirit in her last year and passed away quietly one evening. Our family and Dana, too, had lost the small but fearless leader of our pack.

To lessen our sorrow by keeping us very busy with a puppy, our friends, the St. Johns, gifted us one of their newly born Pug puppies, Alice, who carried the Pug trait of being demanding to an entirely new level. But she lacked Beulah's bearing and Dana completely ignored her ludicrous attempt at tyranny. Self-important but young Alice was not to take that brush-off lightly. Dana, asleep on her back on the family room floor, legs sprawled in all directions, was easy game for Alice, who stormed in and bit Dana's exposed tummy with her needle-like teeth. Oops! With one swipe of the paw, Alice was tumbling across the room, unhurt but wiser. Her curiosity coupled with her greed continually landed her in spaces where she became trapped. We were constantly searching for Alice—in the house, in the yard, in the daytime, at night.

A New Year's Eve tragedy forced Alice to slow down considerably and to accept Dana as her guardian. We had left a reliable teenage neighbor, Liz, to watch Miss Kate and Kurt, the pets and the house while we were at a celebration across the street. Upon returning home in the early morning hours, we immediately noticed that Alice was missing.

"Oh, yeah!" our sitter explained. "When I let out Dana and Alice, the Elkhound next-door jumped her fence and attacked Alice. It was biting, growling and dragging her. I was too frightened to get close to that ferocious dog, but Dana chased her away so I could pick up Alice and carry her into the house. I'm afraid she is dead. I guess I should have called you?"

What emotion most dominated our thoughts—fear, shock, grief, anger, a combination? While Liz was explaining, Wally was putting his face next to Alice, examining her. "She's alive," he whispered. "Try to reach an emergency veterinarian."

None answered their emergency numbers, so Wally, a dentist, used his medical knowledge and suturing abilities to cleanse and close her many teeth-torn, ragged wounds, temporarily stopping the flow of blood. We used our heating pad wrapped in towels to help prevent shock. He worried, "This is New Year's Day. Will we be able to find any help today?"

An emergency veterinarian took our call about eight that morning, and attended to our badly chewed-up Alice for almost an hour. Her midsection, throat, ears, both legs and one eye were covered in bandages, and two drains were inserted. We made her ravaged body as comfortable as possible in a small downstairs room, near the kitchen, where she would not be disturbed, but where we would be able to easily check on her serious condition. For years after, Alice slept curled up next to Dana's warm tummy and refused to go outside without Dana, her new guardian angel.

After we returned with Alice from her long session with the emergency veterinarian, Wally tried to calm his emotions before he made the call to inform our neighbors next-door, but his voice quivered. Having explained the attack and Alice's present condition, he invited Bill and Janet, the owners of the Elkhound-cross, Elkie, to come to our home. They needed to observe, first-hand, the terrible pain and trauma our innocent little Pug was enduring, and the permanent damage their dog had inflicted, unprovoked, in our fenced yard. It was important that they examine today's veterinary charges and the estimate for Alice's continuing care. Their reaction on the phone was neither sympathetic nor apologetic. They were not even solicitous about Alice's condition. To add insult to injury, Bill and Janet coldly refused to walk next-door to our home. Janet stated, in a defensive tone, that if they came, if they visited, or if they even acknowledged Elkie's attack, it would be "admitting guilt."

Wally's response was to the point, truthful and a classic, "Alice was a gift from my best friend, an attorney. I will refer him to you so he can legally explain the seriousness of this situation. I'm sure he will also want to address the current and pending veterinarian charges and any other possible foreseeable damages and well as his legal fees."

We were surprised when cash for the current charges and estimated future procedures were delivered by private courier to Wally's dental office the following day. Inside the generic white envelope with the currency was a note, "Please advise me of further expenses for your dog, Alice. And please do not tell my wife about this transaction." It was signed only with our neighbor's initials.

We filed a written complaint with City Animal Services reporting that our fifteen-pound, young Pug, in her own fenced-in yard, had been viciously attacked and mauled by a neighbor's Elkhound-cross, who jumped over a six-foot fence to reach her. I noted that this aggressive dog would have killed our Pug if it had not been chased away by our Great Dane. We enclosed photos, contact information for Liz as the eyewitness, our attorney, veterinarian, and, of course, the owners of the Elkhound-cross. Elkie was soon moved to an enclosed area in a part of their spacious yard not adjoining ours. This vicious attack on Alice had left her blind in one eye with one disfigured leg that could never quite reach the ground. Her diet was changed permanently to prescription canned-food.

There were to be other unpleasant encounters with these same next door neighbors, Bill and Janet, both physicians. The following summer, while weeding and generally sprucing up the yard for a visit from my in-laws, I spoke with another resident of our neighborhood, Ran, whom I hadn't seen in several years. He was walking, off-leash, a beautiful, very large St. Bernard who was responding without hesitation to his hand and voice controls. When I mentioned how impressed I was, Ran explained that this friendly, white and rust colored dog, which he named Brandy, was left in his yard about three months earlier. He was very fond of Brandy, tried to locate her owner or find a new one. Meanwhile he fed it, made a bed for this majestic giant on his front porch and took a well-trained and beautiful Brandy for morning walks. Because his wife, Thelma, was not a "dog person," Ran stated that she had designated this coming weekend as "when this dog would go."

My father, Pud, with his family's Newfoundland, 1910, Artesia, New Mexico.

The magnificent breeds of St. Bernards and Newfoundlands occupied a very special place in my life. My father's family, in the early 1900s, raised both breeds in Artesia, New Mexico. I assured Ran that I could find a loving, responsible home for this soon-to-be twice-relinquished Saint. Ran and I agreed that as soon as I returned from meeting Wally's parents at the Albuquerque International Airport, locally deemed the Sunport. In a couple of hours I would drive to his home, pick up Brandy and use my resources as education director for Animal Humane Association of New Mexico to relocate her. Our *Albuquerque Journal* and *Albuquerque Tribune* also offered free ads for lost and found pets.

I further explained my situation to Ran. "Until I know how our current household of dogs will react to a new boarder, Wally and I have a large dog run in the back yard where Brandy could stay. We would be more than glad to be temporarily responsible for her care."

Only an hour later, I was opening the back door to leave home for the Sunport. My neighbor to the north, Janet, (oh, yes, *that* neighbor) hollered, "Neighbor! I have Ran's rescued St. Bernard. I have decided to drop her off at Animal Humane."

I tried to control my anxiety. "You know that I volunteer there and am familiar with their policies. They are very limited in the number of kennels that can hold a dog this size. Please wait until I return and I will be sure she is safe, fed, sees a veterinarian and has a good home." Hoping she would heed, I left hurriedly for the Albuquerque's unique Sunport.

It was wonderful to see Wally's parents. Their visit from New Jersey was always a special treat. Having second thoughts about my St. Bernard conversations this morning with my neighbor to the north, I phoned Animal Humane and was told that indeed she had "dropped off" a St. Bernard, but their facility did not have any large kennels available, so they contacted City Animal Services. This information necessitated my explanation to Wally's parents that we would have a slight detour on our trip home.

By the time I was able to "spring" the St. Bernard from Animal Services, my billfold was much lighter due to city fines for an unlicensed, unspayed female dog, running loose. And I had no inoculation records for my "lost dog." In order for the city to release Brandy to me, I had to assume an owner's responsibility for this dog's care.

Paperwork approved and in hand, and Brandy on leash, we finally left the Animal Services building. Once we reached my car, I realized that I was facing yet another challenge in my determination to rescue this dog. How could I fit Brandy into my compact Honda, already crammed with three adults and four well-packed pieces of luggage plus carry-ons? Certainly I would need to move to the trunk their special ordered, made-in-New Jersey deli bag with six tightly-wrapped hoagies, emitting a mouth-watering aroma—too much of a temptation for any dog. I cringed as I hastily pondered this situation. My only solution was to place this humongous, 195-pound canine next to my father-in-law in the already crowded back seat. As feared, on our drive home Brandy shed all over my frustrated father-in-law and slobbered all over the back of my sweet and patient mother-in-law. Her lovely blue suit and newly-coiffed silver hair were both soggy and gooey.

"We are confused because we thought that you only had a Great Dane and a Pug. Wally didn't mention a St. Bernard," they questioned.

Once we reached home, I entered my secluded bedroom and Wally was pre-warned by my phone call to his dental office—he was now aware that we were owners of a

St. Bernard. Our fifteen years of marriage had alerted him, and his staff, that my phone calls to his dental office were usually not about money nor about the children. Mostly they concerned "some rescue animal" in the disdainful words of one of his staff.

Once Wally returned home from the office, his mom and dad continued to voice concern about our growing number of pets. "Wally, why can't you and Kate have only one dog as a family pet, like your sister, Marie, who has a single dog, a Brittany Spaniel, whom her family adores?"

Still, everyone in the family, including his parents, was properly impressed by how well Brandy responded to the training from her previous unknown owner. She was both beautiful and gentle. Sadly, she had not been spayed and probably had to fend for herself for some time before she was found by Ran. That would explain why she was aggressive with other dogs. We could not allow any situation that might lead to a fight between two exceptionally large dogs, Brandy and Dana, each weighing more than 150 pounds.

We made the necessary veterinary and grooming visits. Wally was one proud but busy owner as he took Brandy— after Dana, of course—for daily walks in our neighborhood. Although it was awesome using only hand and vocal signals with Brandy, Wally was still playing it safe by keeping her on leash.

She was an amazing, accomplished animal and was totally enamored with children. After two months of enjoying this magnificent creature while also interviewing prospective owners, we found this giant, furry and loving creature a good home with children, but, as a precautionary measure, without other pets. During the following month, our two house-checks on her new residence had found a dog and family both deliriously happy, which made us deliriously happy, too.

Only a few months would pass before we were called upon to care for other needy pets—four newborn multicolored kittens after the sudden death of their mother. Our utility room bath served as their home, and Wally and I took shifts throughout the evening and early morning hours with the eyedropper and infant formula recommended by our veterinarian. Feeding them was a painful experience for Wally. In their frenzied search for nourishment, they were showing no mercy as they clawed up his pajama legs. Those torturous actions earned them special names from Wally: Adolph, Tojo, Benito and Fidel.

My job had a great deal of latitude, so they became my responsibility from 8 to 5. I carted them to my office and reconnected their heating pad in their hidden-under-my-desk, small, zip-up crate. Only occasional eyedropper feedings (in a ladies' room stall) interrupted their sound sleeping throughout my working day. When the kittens were finally weaned, at about six weeks old, it was Dana who assumed the "mothering" duties: providing protection, keeping them warm and clean, and corralling those that roamed out of range. A 160-pound dog tenderly caring for kittens, each weighing less than one pound was a wondrous site! *What if we humans would demonstrate that same indiscriminate compassion—no prejudice with a "regardless of" attitude?*

Dana wore many hats in our family, from tenderly mothering helpless kittens to embarrassing our insecure children with her canine habits. It was mortifying experience for our two mid-school children to ride in the front seat of the family Buick with their mother while Dana's sprawl enveloped the back seat, and streaks of her saliva swirled on all back windows. My yellow-rimmed sunglasses were another source of constant embarrassment for them, my cue to increase their discomfort. So I purchased and placed an almost-identical pair of yellow sunglasses on Dana, then I picked-up the kids from school in the family Buick. I honked to capture the attention of their classmates to our matching snazzy eyewear. What a shocking response from the "embarrassed" duo as they tried not to acknowledge our presence! What a cool canine! What a hoot!

One hat Dana wore and earned, about which we were surprised, was that of protector. As I did my gardening on the south side of our home both Alice and Dana enjoyed lying next to me, not as protectors, but as sun-worshipers— on their backs, tummies exposed, taking in the rays. But as I dug my spade into the soil, one quiet sunny, summer afternoon, without warning, a low guttural growl emitted from Dana's throat and off she took, long gaits covering the grounds quickly. By the time I reached her by the north gate, she had already attacked a cable service man, who still held the gate lock-cutters in his hand. The severed lock lay on the ground. He lay sprawled on the ground, hand at his neck, bleeding profusely. Dana was growling, positioned horizontally between us in a protective stance, unmoving. The moment was tense; I was terrified as I cried out, "Ohhhhhh, wwwhat?"

"Lady, I was in a hurry and didn't want to walk around your property to connect your neighbor's cable, so I cut your gate lock to get to the utility pole. I didn't know you actually had a dog. Everyone has those '*Beware of Dog*' signs and usually they have no dog." He too was frightened, and remained on the ground, not daring to move for fear of Dana.

I raced inside to first phone 911 and then our attorney, who assured us that, because our gates were substantial, locked, posted, and Dana had no history of violence, we were safe from the legalities that might arise from this unfortunate incident. He knew his law. If cutting locks on a customer's property in order to gain access had been an unwritten policy of the cable company, I hoped that this almost-tragic episode changed their reckless trespassing.

At ten years old, our precious, protective Dana developed "bloat" and within less than an hour, she died. This condition is one of the most serious health problems of Danes and is caused by the stomach filling with an excess of fluids and gas. Usually this results in the stomach twisting, and death. No conclusive data answers why this is a cause of death in more than forty percent of Great Danes.

We thought Dana was more intuitive and more understanding than any dog we had ever owned. Her sensibility and responsible behavior could admonish us with just a look. Her dignity, elegance, stature and strength depicted the regal beast that she was. These many admirable characteristics along with her calm, kind but watchful manner earned her the title of "Our Great One."

Uncle Bill with Buffy and friends Misty and Motley.

CHAPTER 10

BUFFY AND FRIENDS

"Until one has loved an animal, a part of one's soul remains unawakened."

— **Anatole France**

Our family took Dana's death with great difficulty. Without her, Alice seemed lost and was always trailing after us, always underfoot. With Dana gone, which of us was going to protect her, because now she was physically disabled, partially blind and apprehensive?

My friend Josie at the City Animal Services phoned a few months later. "I have the perfect dog for your family, to help with your loss of Dana. An owner-surrender, red-and-white boxer pup was just brought in because, as her annoyed owner stated, 'She got herself pregnant.'

"It is because of this condition that we at the shelter plan to euthanize her, unless, of course, you want her." Our whole family was there within the hour, getting our new Boxer a city license, inoculations, and signing paperwork to have her spayed immediately. Because of her sleek and athletic-looking body, the kids suggested we name her Buffy.

Buffy was young, exceptionally sweet and so very happy to be in our home. She loved everyone at first sight, even Alice. And because Buffy was the opposite of Alice, pleasing us was her delight. Her cute, stubby tail constantly wagged the rest of her body. Her soft, brown and pleading eyes made her easy to spoil. To our surprise, our newly acquired pooch seemed to recognize Alice's physical impairments and chose to stay close to her.

One summer afternoon Kurt and his across-the-street pal, Stevie, entered the house with Cheshire grins, ear to ear, and a Valvoline Oil box that was bouncing. "How much do you love me, Mom?" Inside was a beautiful but very frightened and small Papillion-cross, a small French-origin pup about fifteen-pounds. Her slender dainty legs were tightly and painfully tied together with a scratchy henna rope.

"Someone threw her, all tied-up, out of their car into the vacant lot next to the Chevron station. We had to rescue her. The service station gave us this box so we could carry her home. Do you think she is hurt?"

Gently we untied and examined her. She didn't appear to be injured, but you could feel her body shaking through her very long, fine and silky coat, white with golden patches. As expected, she was matted and dirty, and apparently her roll from the car had landed her in a bed of goatheads. These are little, sharp, multi-thorned, ground-hugging weeds commonly found in New Mexico. A skillful groomer could take care of that nasty problem. Surprisingly she didn't snap, or whine or growl. What a brave little dog! She wasn't frightened at all, not of us or of any of "our guys." She was confident, friendly and ready to play, after gulps of water and a Pup-Peroni. I was mesmerized by her immediate trust and constant attention. Our "Dogs Found" ad in the *Albuquerque Journal* produced no phone calls. Because she was partial to me, it was my privilege to name her: Misty.

We became inseparable. If she wasn't seated next to me, she was peeking from my pocket. But when her dainty little feet hit the ground, they were zipping here, zipping there. We laughed at her antics and called her our "Zippity-Do-Da Dog." Always the escape artist, Misty, one short year later, dug under our wooden fence and darted into the dangerous, speeding traffic that still, almost thirty years later, continues negligently unchecked by our local police department. It was a fatal and heartbreaking incident.

An owner-surrender, energetic red Cocker Spaniel puppy, Whiskey, was our next charge. I received an imploring call from the dog's owner, a student of mine at Rio Grande Zoo. Kurt picked him up and brought him home, taking a detour to a nearby McDonald's, "because he looked so unhealthy, so haggard, Mother."

In no time at all Whiskey had Kurt "wrapped" and was sharing his twin bed with his other canine buddies, Motley and Buddy. Whiskey was perky, mischievous and beyond cute. And with regular, balanced meals, supplemented by Kurt's occasional cuisine from Mickey D's (hold the onions), he grew into an extremely happy, healthy and handsome animal. His long red, wavy coat glowed as he pranced daily around the wooden and chain link fences enclosing the back yard, but always carrying some adornment in his mouth.

Whiskey enjoyed our apple tree.

Apples from our tree, flowers from our garden or a tissue from the house were his favorite choices. Although if we were careless, he proudly sported a leather garden glove.

What a clown! We were only allowed a few years to laugh at his antics and enjoy his love before a ruptured spleen brought a quick and tragic end to our charming Whiskey's active life.

We were now responsible for four dogs and two cats. Obviously taking trips as a family was becoming more difficult because one of our two trusted pet-sitters had to be booked very early. Only once were we not fortunate enough in our scheduling. During Kurt's junior year in high school, his skill as a gifted sprinter qualified him for the Junior Olympics held at Hofstra University in Long Island, NY. We were exceptionally proud of his accomplishment; our trip to New York would be exciting and we could cheer him to victory. But at the last minute, our scheduled house-and-pet-sitter became ill and would not be able to honor her commitment. Our second sitter was not available. While I remained at home, Wally and his best friend, Uncle Bill, were able to make the trip to watch Kurt as he dashed across the finish line.

In 1984 our resident list grew in a new way, as did our major responsibilities. Now included, besides our two children and a variety of rescue dogs, were our two delightful New Jersey nieces, living with us while studying and changing majors at the University of New Mexico. The oldest, Kim, was gifted by a hopeful boyfriend, a devoted, flat-faced but smiling, red with black mask Pekingese, whom she named BamBam. This breed of toy dogs dates back to more than 2,000 years ago in Western China. Kim's descendant of this ancient breed was only nine pounds but strong-willed and spoiled. When Kim was home, those big bright eyes worked their charm and BamBam's short, bowed legs never touched the ground, but when Kim was at school, BamBam was happy waddling behind the Buffy-Alice team.

Unable to sleep one night, I followed an offending, loud noise to Kim and Elaine's bedroom and discovered that these annoying sniffling and snoring sounds were coming from the Pekingese nose of little BamBam. Kim, who liked to dazzle us with her medical terminology, explained, "Aunt Kate, that snoring is because this breed has an inherent condition termed brachycephaly."

Quickly Kim learned that pets, even adorable pets such as BamBam, require scheduled care. Sunday afternoons were specifically set aside for the grooming of her dog's profuse coat, brushing BamBam's small, sharp teeth, and consistent obedience training. More often than not, procrastination changed those good intentions. These best-laid plans could not always be realized with Kim's busy study and operatory schedule in UNM's Dental Hygiene School, where she flourished and her grades excelled.

The many great qualities of our five dogs—BamBam, Alice, Misty and Kurt's dog, Motley—were no match for Buffy's reliability and tenderness. Today, more than twenty years later, both nieces have chosen rescued Boxers, because of their docile, dependable and loving nature, for their family pets. Their Boxers—Mahler, Cloe and Sadie—like Buffy, just want to please...anyone. And today, gluttons for punishment, we still continue to happily endure the bossy and stubborn personality traits of Pugs and tend to the physical ailments associated with sweet Cocker Spaniels.

Motley's devotion to Kurt lasted until his final breaths.

CHAPTER 11

MOTLEY'S ULTIMATE GIFT

"He is your friend, your partner, your defender, your dog. You are his life, his love, his leader. He will be yours, faithful and true, to the last beat of his heart. You owe it to him to be worthy of such devotion."

– Anonymous

Within months of entering high school as a freshman, Kurt brought home a cuddly Samoyed, Motley Crue. *Who else but a teenage boy would name a sweet, innocent dog after a notorious, loud and heavy-metal rock group?*

Motley's admission into our family was preceded by a week of finagling by Kurt. "Mom, Dad," he said in his saddest, most serious voice, "this poor little white puppy keeps following me when I leave the campus. He just waits for me. I am sure he does not belong to anyone. Do you think we could keep him?"

"Is he following you because you are giving him treats, Kurt?" we asked.

"Well, yes, I did sneak him a few doughnuts. I could tell that he was starved. He needs a home where his owners will feed him nutritional food." He continued this concocted story while our eyebrows and smiles were raised to the extreme.

How can you snicker quietly?

It was weeks later, after Motley was firmly entrenched at our home that we uncovered the true "low-down." Kurt had actually purchased Motley. He raised the asking price, 100 dollars, by selling his video games to a nearby pawn shop, with the help of his classmate's cousin. (Pawn shops require that you are twenty-one.) This "poor little lost puppy" had a breeder, who lived near the high school campus, and had invited several of the students to his garage to view his newest litter of Samoyed puppies. Kurt chose Motley "because he waddled straight to me, Mom." It was Kurt's first experience of being in debt beyond his means, as his weekly stipend for household chores was five dollars.

Motley became not only a handsome, alert and very

patient dog, but Kurt's most loyal buddy. However, when Kurt was not at home, this well-behaved dog could really get into—and get our other dogs into—big, bad trouble.

Puppy Motley and Misty were continually at play.

Even though a six-foot wooden-slat fence enclosed our almost two acres, Motley found that the way "out" was "under." He would dig the hole; then he and Buffy would scramble under and embark on a new adventure on the outside-the-fence world. To thwart their escape, we were always reinforcing the bottom of that fence with heavy, eight-foot railroad ties wrapped in chicken wire, which we buried and stapled to the wooden crossbars of fence. Our final touches were large boulders and native prickly pear cacti, which we intertwined in the wire. It was an inventive but unsuccessful labor as we were still chasing after Buffy and Motley to nearby horse corrals, where they would be gleefully rolling in, and therefore covered with, horse manure. Once both escapees were found and safely in our back seat, the ride home, although less than a mile, with the windows down, was "scentful."

A year later Buffy learned her lesson the hard way. Although she was only grazed by a quickly braking car and suffered only minor injuries that required but a few stitches near her left eye, she became wary of the road. With no one to dig escape tunnels for, Motley quickly lost interest in his excavations. What a relief for us ... no more contraptions to build, no more holes to fill, no more dogs to chase!

On weekend mornings, Kurt, a teenager, would sleep late, surrounded in bed by Buffy, Motley and Whiskey. Wally would open Kurt's bedroom door early in the morning to allow the dogs to go outside to relieve themselves. Anxious, pent-up, legs almost crossed, Buffy and Whiskey leaped out of his bed and scurried outside, but Motley would never leave Kurt. That mirrored their relationship of an unshakable bond for twelve years.

What a tragic day it was when Motley was diagnosed with a very progressive cancer of the lymph nodes. Kurt's devastation was in his voice. "I have made the decision to keep him at home until we are ready to schedule his final veterinarian appointment. Motley and I need closure time together."

Because Motley was very ill, Kurt and Motley slept for months, side by side, on the outside patio, regardless of the weather. Kurt's insect bites were large and so multiple that they resembled chicken pox. A few spider bites were so swollen and painful that Wally was forced to use his surgical skills to lance and drain them, as gently as possible.

Months later, Motley's terminal condition had

worsened. Kurt called the veterinarian to make his final appointment. The following day, at noon, Wally, Kurt and I left work and arrived at home. Kurt gently carried Motley to his car. On the trip to the vets, Motley expired, sparing Kurt that ultimate heart-wrenching responsibility at the veterinarian's office. Motley, along with Alice, Whiskey, Misty, Dana, Buffy and many others of our most cherished pets, is buried on our special Plot of Pets in the back yard, where they once played together.

Several years would pass before Kurt would choose another canine companion in 2007. His present dog, a smart, spoiled-by-love, beautiful black Labrador Retriever, Ella, became his constant companion, his most loyal friend. Their strong bond epitomized that undying loyalty, which authors attempt and fail to capture, one so deep that it cannot be explained with mere words.

Kurt and Ella enjoyed exploring the mountains in the snow.

Although a few of our other dogs, Babes and Rex had very expressive faces, Ella was one of the few dogs whose face would always reveal her emotions. One of her most ridiculous reactions was when she screwed up her forehead, eyes and muzzle, then turned her head in disgust when one of "the guys" had an accident in the house and had peed on the floor. Her "above it all" attitude and tendency to be a tattler did not endear Ella to "our guys." Kurt had yet to tell her that she, too, was a dog. She would never believe him.

However, in case of an outbreak of canine bickering, she would assert her dictatorial personality and become our peacemaker. Ella was the easiest, most dependable dog we have ever had in the family. Whenever her life would become a bit boring, she, at seventy pounds, just had to steal a stuffed animal from our twenty-two-pound Peaches. Ella had no desire to play with the toy; she did this only for Peaches' reaction. Poor Peaches would run to me, incensed, with small cries revealing she was helpless. "That big black bully has my stuffy."

Ella readily gave it back to me and smiled. Yes, she actually gave a wide toothy grin. I handed her toy back to Peaches, but, "Yuck! It is soaked with Ella's slobber." Peaches dropped it, refusing it until it had dried. It was all in a day of play.

The unwavering, dependable and admirable behavior of Kurt's wonderful, exciting and aware companion, Ella, exemplified the reason why Labrador Retrievers had remained, for more than ten years, the number-one dog registered by AKC pet owners. It was surprising that a Labrador had never won the "Best of Show" title in the annual Westminster Dog Show. But this brilliant (she could turn on our outside water-spigot), perceptive and obedient dog won "Best of Dogdom" in Kurt's eyes. She was as totally committed to Kurt as he was to her.

Muffin was a determined beauty with a mind of her own.

CHAPTER 12

MOST PRECIOUS PERFECT

"Being spoiled by a dog is entering a love-lived life."

Wally was awakened in bed on the morning of his fiftieth birthday with a lick and the amazing, unique smell of puppy. Miss Kate, our daughter, had presented him a curly, blonde, precious and precocious Cocker Spaniel. In fact, my first words upon seeing her were, "Oh, most precious!"

To which Wally quickly added, "Perfect." Thus her name, established within minutes, was Most Precious Perfect. Our kids, easily embarrassed teens, just called her "Muffin." Find a flattering adjective and we would apply it to Muffin. Whether it referred to her appearance or behavior, we were oblivious. With her big brown eyes, soft, fluffy coat and puppy ways, this blonde had us "wrapped." When she was not receiving her due adoration, she would sit nearby, lift her curly head up to the skies and give us her long, howling, "Woooo-woooo." This was her signal for attention, for play, to be wooed. Her perks were without limits. Although we scoffed at our children ever having their photos taken with

"What am I doing here?"

Santa, Muffin posed with him on her first Christmas. We were so enamored with this canine juvenile delinquent that no one even considered using the "No" word.

A neighbor's sarcastic comment describing Muffin as "the beauty and the beast" got my attention. No more lollygagging around. It was time to take positive, no-non-sense steps. I scheduled her, as I had for all of our dogs, in obedience classes. But it was Wally who insisted that, because she was his birthday gift, it was his duty to attend those classes. What a fiasco! She (and Wally) actual-ly failed their first session, so when they enrolled in their second try at novice-obedience, I trailed along uninvited, of course. The problem was evident. Wally was just not a disciplinarian. With his soft-spoken and gentle manner, he was directing Muffin, "Now, Precious, you need to sit." Or, he would continue, "Little Muffin, please sit." There was no authority inflected in his voice. Since obedience school is meant to train both the dog and its owner, this training class was definitely doomed. She was our only dog to fail obedience classes—twice. Yet she became the brave and adventurous alpha of all of "the guys."

Muffin was so agile that she could jump from the back of our family-room couch to a nearby barstool. By bounc-ing up and down on the barstool, she then turned it so that she was facing the breakfast bar, where all prepared food was placed. After enjoying the *fare du jour* presented, she would quickly exit back to the couch, via barstool, in the same manner. Until we caught her in this action, the whole family was puzzled, blaming one another, for the disappear-ance of various foods, which we knew that we had placed on the bar.

We no more than moved the barstools from their convenient spot at the breakfast bar than our food-motivated monster would devise a new stunt. By running across the kitchen, hitting and bouncing off the door of our refrigerator, she could spring it open.

You could read her mind. *"Oh! The culinary choices inside the fridge are much more varied and much greater than the breakfast bar!"* And, after she savored our leftovers, she left the refrigerator door open for us to close.

Logically we should have been suspicious, finding the refrigerator door open, but it seemed that, even when faced with the obvious, we were without sleuthing skills. So once again, Muffin's family pled guilty to being completely perplexed.

"Whoever forgot to close the refrigerator door should be made to clean up when Muffin is sick all night." No one fessed up.

"Who was responsible?" was an unanswered question.

"Who? Me"?

Our Three Muskateers were a hoot!

Finally Kurt's midnight snack trip to the kitchen caught Muffin in her athletic endeavor. Now that we were wiser, realizing that our Most Precious Perfect was the culprit, we were both apologetic and embarrassed. We wrapped the refrigerator door with wide strips of electrical tape, inconveniently having to re-tape after each opening. Although our newly silver-striped refrigerator could not considered to be a one of the designer projects advertised to update a kitchen, it certainly improved the edibility and availability of the food stored inside our refrigerator.

One summer we decided to take Miss Kate and Kurt on a five-day adventure to Disneyland. Our new pet and house sitter, Louise, met our five dogs: a Pug, Babes; three Cocker Spaniels we called the "Three Musketeers"— Muffin, Whiskey and Rusty—and Brady, a black-and-white Parti Cocker Spaniel.

We instructed Louise that all of our dogs were fairly easy to manage, but sweet-looking Muffin had the hidden talents of a master criminal. Louise listened carefully, but we could tell by her inattentive attitude that she had discounted (as bragging?) our stories about Muffin's prowess. On our second evening away, we phoned Louise for an update. Her exasperated tone on the telephone revealed that her original assessment of Muffin's ingenuity had been underrated.

"Last night after dinner I put my leftover roast beef with mushrooms in the refrigerator. This morning the door was open. The roast was gone. Muffin does not like mushrooms," she tartly replied.

One time we failed to completely close the door to the dog food bin and found her by the open

Muffin discovers the appeal of a Christmas tree.

door, hunkered down, her short, sturdy body seemingly glued to the floor. She was gobbling and storing the morsels in her cheeks as she furiously continued to gorge. She had made her small body so stiff that it was almost impossible to move her. To describe Muffin as "food-oriented" would be an understatement. It was because she could easily outsmart her dull family that she was always being placed on a diet.

It was impossible to predict her next caper. So while we were busy arming the house with childproof locks, slide-bolt latches and doorknobs to replace our designer door handles, she was busy chewing out jacket pockets that contained gum (sugar-free) and learning to turn and open those newly installed doorknobs. She particularly enjoyed that special taste of my mother-in-law's Kenneth Cole leather gloves… twice. Suffice to say, such nibbling was not well received.

That type of agility and curiosity was bound to find its owner in trouble. And trouble was what Muffin found when she was able to jump onto the bathroom counter and open our medicine cabinet. We were fortunate that I discovered her after only half of the 100-tablet jar of Aleve had been ingested. The veterinarians at the emergency clinic labored for hours on our Most Precious Perfect. Much to the surprise of the clinic staff, she survived and was responding to their expert and tender treatment. Daily at 8:30 a.m. I would arrive and be ushered to her cement-floored kennel in their critical-care unit.

I came prepared with a thermos of freshly brewed coffee, a small, thick rug on which to sit and a book, from which I would read out loud to Muffin. On her fifth day in the veterinarian hospital, a weekend, Wally accompanied me. Because of two prior emergencies, the staff informed us there would be a considerable wait before we could visit Muffin. It was several hours later when a vet-tech led us back to her kennel. She was still listless and still encumbered with IVs attached to tubes, which were attached to monitors. However, she was so spoiled and angry with us for our unacceptable tardiness that she stood up from her bed and, legs wobbling, walked away from us to her kennel gate, which faced a blank, gray concrete wall. Muffin would not even acknowledge our presence with a wag. This was not frustrating. It was funny. It was a relief. Her giving us the cold shoulder was almost human. We took it as a sign than she was definitely feeling better.

She recovered from that very close brush with death.

As a coming-home-from-the-hospital gift, we found a brown, furry hedgehog stuffed toy in the clinic's pet shop. We could not have chosen a better-received toy. Hedgie was carried everywhere by Muffin, and not shared with the other dogs or other humans either… ever.

Four years later I was awakened early one wintry morning by telltale noises of Muffin becoming ill. As I carefully carried her down the dark, seven concrete steps to our back yard, I slipped and took a hard fall down the steps, surviving with only lacerations, bruises and a broken ankle. My guardian angel was working overtime. Muffin landed unscathed.

Age and glaucoma did not damper Muffin's determination, as, up to her fifteenth birthday bash (complete with a photo cake and twenty guests), she was still plotting and often successfully executing maneuvers for which we were still ill-prepared. We were never a match for this manipulative, ingenuous and most precious, perfect creature!

Muffin and Sammy's Fifteenth Birthday Cake was picture-perfect.

Rusty Radar, although blind, was a tough trekker.

CHAPTER 13

RUSTY RADAR

"Any society which does not insist upon respect for all life must necessarily decay."

– Albert Einstein

In 1997, a blind, thirty-two-pound, older Cocker Spaniel-Chow Chow cross was left by his owner in the middle of the interchange of Interstate 25 and Interstate 40 in Albuquerque. He was rescued from the speeding and dangerous highway traffic by a brave and kind Public Service Company of New Mexico (PNM) work crew member. He had actually observed this throw-away canine being carried out of a pickup truck and dumped on the interchange.

Thinking that any animal shelter would find him a home, the PNM employee took him by a nearby rescue facility, completed the required paperwork and left, confident that the dog would soon be enjoying a loving home. Sadly, this caring man could not have been more mistaken, for at that time, the heartbreaking but necessary policy at the shelter was to euthanize all unlicensed pets who were physically impaired and old. Their kennels and those of other rescue groups were in a constant state of overflow, full of too many young and healthy adoptable dogs and cats. Their policy, though harsh, was a realistic adaptation to the sad state of abandoned animals in our state.

Because of Angel, my kindred contact at the shelter, we were accepted as this dog's foster family the very afternoon that he was admitted. He was mellow, quiet, easy-to-love and anxious to return that love. His color became his name, Rusty.

Within the month, Angel and I found him a permanent home in Portales, New Mexico, located in the eastern part of the state. One week later, Rusty was returned because the new owner's two dogs showed aggression toward him, which can sometimes be the case with a weaker, disabled animal. Angel felt so strongly about this amazing dog that she drove the entire 486-mile trip to and from Portales to bring Rusty back to our home. That dedication earned her the title, Rusty's Guardian Angel. With tears of joy, and a couple of homemade cheese balls, we welcomed him back into our menagerie, for good. I completed the official adoption papers on the following day and Rusty became a permanent member of "the guys."

Our friends and family always seemed interested when we would acquire a newly rescued or adopted pet. However, after a tennis game at the courts across the street, Wally was explaining how thrilled we were with our new dog, Rusty. One of Wally's team members blurted out, in an irreverent tone, "Why do you keep such a dog, blind and old?"

Wally didn't hesitate, "Because we have been given the chance to make up for his previous life."

It was understandable that because of his age, background and blindness, Rusty interacted with our other dogs by ignoring them. Sensing when one of us was upset or ill, he huddled next to us for hours, guarding us from unknown present or future misfortunes. He was our first totally unselfish dog.

With a solid and steady gait, he lumbered around our property. Rusty enjoyed and excelled at the surefooted hiking skills required to explore our nearly two-acre fenced grounds of rugged terrain. In spite of being blind, he climbed daily up and down steep rocky hills, ravines, through prickly shrubs, around cacti, through both a run-off and a stream and returned to the house with his coat still clean and dry. What a GPS he had! These incredible tracking talents, for a blind dog, earned him the handle, Rusty Radar!

One winter evening six years later, just as it was becoming dusk, Wally and I were puzzled as Rusty had not returned from his rounds. Armed only with the beam of our flashlight, Wally searched the treacherous and icy terrain in the back, and took a ten-foot fall down a steep, rocky slope. Twelve hours and an emergency hospital visit later, we were relieved that only a painful fourteen stitches on his scalp were necessary. No bones were broken.

That next morning, Rusty, whom, in the excitement of Wally's tumble, we had completely forgotten, appeared at our back door, limping, muddy and bloody. The veterinarian's observations revealed that he was slowly losing his hearing, the remaining sense on which he heavily depended for his daily routine. With each passing month, Rusty became more and more despondent. He was no longer capable of reconnoitering through the back yard without incident. Now Rusty is buried in our back yard, where his spirit can continue to track, unimpaired. Rusty was one of our greatest dogs, a true and gentle gent.

Because of our city's overflow of discarded pets, Rusty's future could have ended tragically on that fateful afternoon that he was impounded. Almost ten years after the rescue of Rusty, our city adopted a much more humane ordinance regulating euthanasia in our kennels. In response to the hundreds of pets picked up monthly by the city and never reclaimed, in response to the astronomical euthanasia rates of impounded animals in our kennels, and in response to the hundreds of animal-cruelty cases a year, our city, through the actions of one city councilor, acted.

In 2006, our city passed an outstanding, up-to-date, sixty-eight page ordinance, HEART (Humane and Ethical

Animal Rules and Treatment), authored by City Councilor Sally Mayer. It required that all pets be chipped and registered with a city license. Owners of more than four dogs must apply for and be investigated before being given a multiple-animal permit, and their property, both inside and outside, is to be inspected by city animal welfare officers.

This ordinance also states that all dogs and cats older than six months must be spayed or neutered, excepting those whose guardians possess a special intact permit. Yes, Albuquerque still had illegal breeders who sold or gave away puppies without the required license or permit, but our HEART ordinance was a positive preventive measure to ensure healthier care for many of our area pets.

There was difficulty in discovering and fining those illegal breeders as well as the irresponsible owners who had many animals beyond the allowable number, because they never contacted animal services for licenses and a permit. If pet owners failed to license their animals, their pets seldom had the required permanent chipping. When these dogs or cats were lost or thrown away, there was no license, no chipping or identification linking the pet to an owner. The probability of finding the actual owner was miniscule. The probability of their meeting with misfortune or being euthanized was almost a given. These conditions describe many of the rescues that had, during the past fifty years, come to our doorstep.

Pets are too often discarded by irresponsible owners, like a Kleenex tissue, disposable. Their owners' pitiful excuses covered a broad band of believability. Possibly their owners were moving, or developed allergies to pets, or were unable financially to care for the pet, or didn't like the pet anymore, or didn't have time to train the pet, or found a better pet, or were pregnant, or couldn't keep the dog from barking or peeing in the house or scratching at the door or jumping on people. The dog "grew up," or "kissed too much," or "didn't bark enough," or "was too active," or "couldn't catch the ball," or "wanted too much attention" or "shed too much." In short, these pet owners found ludicrous excuses because they no longer wanted to accept the responsibility of caring for their dog or cat, a pet that was once a member of their household. Could the reason that the numbers of these castaways is not decreasing, but increasing, be due to our more negligent, irresponsible society?

The recently released impound numbers from our hard-working and concerned Albuquerque Animal Welfare Department (AAWD) were heartbreaking. These figures revealed that our city animal shelters were so overcrowded (more than 14,900 dogs impounded in 2012) that it necessitated housing the overflow in garages (527 pets were brought in during one week alone.). This deplorable condition gave birth to the innovative and successful "Free Dog Weekend," sponsored by a frustrated AAWD. It was patterned after a similar event for cats, previously held, in which AAWD reported that 101 felines found new homes. These fee-waived pets offered by AAWD were sterilized, inoculated, micro-chipped and given a voucher for a free veterinarian's visit.

Regrettably (*What adverb can adequately describe this?*) the private, county and city shelters in Albuquerque still euthanize approximately 9,000 healthy and treatable animals each year. And in the United States, it is estimated that between 4,000,000 and 12,000,000 healthy, adoptable pets are euthanized annually. Pet owners must not turn a deaf ear to this painful plight and slaughter of abandoned, unwanted dogs and cats.

What if we used our involvement in community organizations—Boy Scouts, Girl Scouts, Camp Fire Boys and Girls, YMCA, YWCA…the list is endless—to educate young pet owners. If most dog owners were made aware that one unspayed dog can be responsible for the birth of more than 100 puppies in just two years, could we convince them to spay or neuter their dog? If most cat owners were made aware that cats have a rapid breeding rate and just one unspayed cat can be responsible for the birth of more than fifty kittens in only sixteen short months, could we convince them to spay or neuter their cat? And I cite a last, important "if."

If most pet owners in America—there are a great number of us—would make a monthly donation of money, earmarked for sterilization, or spend time volunteering at one of their local shelters, we pet owners as a group could make and should make (it is our responsibility) a difference in this deplorable situation, this senseless slaughter yearly of millions of dogs and cats. If more companion animals could be sterilized, fewer litters would result. Fewer litters would result in fewer strays. Fewer strays mean less euthanasia. That is a simple, workable plan that even the busiest pet owner can follow…but we have to care enough about the suffering in their lives to incorporate this plan in our own individual, busy schedules. Ninety-eight percent of Americans consider pets to be their beloved companions or cherished members of the family. Now is the time for us to prove it by donating our energies, resources and monies to help put a halt to these senseless deaths, the result of unchecked breeding.

We also have the responsibility to tighten the spaying and neutering ordinances in our communities, counties and states. By using the Internet, it is easy to compare yours with successful ones in other areas. While on the Internet, also check the scope of the laws or ordinances in your particular state, county and community that will protect your pet (particularly if it is lost) as well as those pets who are victims of abuse. I found my area shelters and rescue groups to have pertinent and up-to-date knowledge about these laws. I also relied on bulletins from Animal Protection Voters (a branch of Animal Protection of New Mexico), whose motto is "We change the laws that change their lives." Nationally, the Humane Society of the United States has always presented a strong, ongoing force against animal cruelty, exploitation and neglect.

By comparing your researched facts and statistics to those of other states, you can determine if they are strong enough to give the pets in your area the safety and respect they deserve, which includes affordable spaying and neutering. Is animal cruelty or extreme animal cruelty appropriately designated as a felony or merely as a misdemeanor? Is there cooperation between your animal welfare officers and the court? Do your laws and ordinances have the educated manpower to enforce them? How did your present legislatures vote on recently introduced animal-humane bills? Which cities have animal-humane or sterilization legislation that your community could use as models? Which of your city councilors, state or federal legislators are known for their compassion on animal legislation?

Lavaland ES students learn about responsible dog ownership, the need to spay/neuter and the proper care of animals from Kate Kuligowski and other volunteers from the Animal Humane Association who make individual class presentations to students. Kate, a former teacher, has developed a K-12 curriculum dealing with animal issues.

– Albuquerque Public Schools Newsletter: *Perspective*, Feb. 7, 2000

Chapter 14

YOU AND YOUR PET
ARE FOREVER

"The only way you can change the way people think about and behave towards their pets, and all animals, is through education."

My decision to volunteer as education director for Animal Humane Association of New Mexico (AHANM), now AHNM, from 1997 to 2002 was motivated by an atrocious incident which occurred while we were walking Muffin and Motley in a park near our home. Also enjoying this park was a young family with three children under the age of ten with their three, unleashed, small and fluffy white dogs. Their impatient attempts to teach obedience to their dogs resulted in actual temper tantrums: yelling, hitting and even kicking at their pets, who were yelping, running away and cowering from their owners.

It was impossible for me to watch this cruel situation without interfering. I approached them and introduced myself. Using our dogs to explain some easy basics of training, I had the attention of these eager children as, together, we taught their little dogs to "sit" and "come." The parents, however, made no secret of their disinterest, and without acknowledging me or my efforts, gruffly packed up the kids and pets, and departed.

The following morning, with a desire to make a difference in pet care education, I spoke on the phone with the Joel Levy, director of AHANM, who explained that they had no education department because they lacked the funding. I voiced my belief that, "The only way you can change the way people think about and behave toward their pets, and all animals, is through education. Pertinent information, presented in an interesting and exciting manner can give their whole family a better understanding of responsible animal care, thus giving their pet the chance of a fuller life."

My experience as a former classroom teacher in grades

K-12, Education Curator for the Rio Grande Zoo in Albuquerque, and program and education coordinator for Camp
Fire Boys and Girls provided excellent credentials for such
a position with this organization. After the interview in his
office, the director assigned my duties as the AHANM volunteer education director: to visit classrooms and civic
organizations across the state, teaching a pre-approved program of humane education. Less than $100 yearly would
be approved and available for this new program. I would
have to beg, borrow and scramble for everything additional
that my program would require.

After a month of intense research and interviews and
inquiries, I named my program, *"You and Your Pet Are
Forever."* For the use of our state's classroom teachers,
I published two humane education instruction manuals,
with that title, for grades K-5 and 6-12, both including activity sheets, lesson plans, research projects and timely topics
for discussion or debate. With the expertise of AHANM
employees, two slide shows with sound were made to complement the nine chosen videos from the director's library.
I scheduled, by phone, classroom visits in the Greater
Albuquerque area as well as with those towns within a
250-mile radius of here.

The main message of the program was tender and
responsible pet care. As we discussed different types of pet
foods, I emphasized those specific foods which, if ingested,
could be especially dangerous to a pet's health: alcohol, avo-
cado, chocolate, coffee, garlic, grapes, onions, raisins and, of
course, spicy leftovers. A great deal of time was devoted to
the importance of spaying and neutering their pets, which
would result in fewer pets being euthanized. Those who

questioned this teaching were quick to explain that their pet was the prettiest, most handsome, smartest, sweetest, etc. I countered, "No, my dog is…the smartest, most talented, etc. We all feel that way, because it is a natural emotion for all loving pet owners to believe that theirs is the best."

I held three-day classes for volunteer teachers in our locale. Our number of dependable volunteers for the program fluctuated between four and six. One of AHANM's educational volunteers, Kris Keller, showed such dedication, perseverance and energy that she topped 300 classroom hours in only one year before returning to APS as a full-time art teacher.

"You And Your Pet Are Forever" needed a child magnet, a super-star of my road show, a real live dog. AHANM arranged that I could make my choice, each day, from the many abandoned or surrendered dogs from the kennels in each community where I was scheduled. My first day of teaching was in a nearby rural community, Sandstone. I arrived at their shelter early and there chose a female dog, who had been abandoned on the road with her recently born, dead puppies. She had an excellent temperament, lapped up the attention, and was, therefore, easy to train to "sit, come and down." Although her appearance screamed, "cur," her eagerness to please and her constantly wagging tail made her adorable. She resembled so many other dogs that you see in shelters: medium-sized, short yellow hair, long tail, long nose, big brown eyes. Her teats, still large from recently giving birth, hung. I named her Kleenex, because she had been used, then discarded.

Because she was very friendly and learned easily, Kleenex and my program were a hit in all the classrooms I visited on my first day. Students, teachers and parents, too, were amazed that such a cur could outperform their own household pets. The lesson of spending quality time with your pet was quickly understood because of her example. These classrooms were learning that how well a dog behaved depended not so much on the breed, but usually on the owner. This same line of thinking is constantly cited by owners of the often-outlawed breed, Pit Bull Terriers.

When I returned, late afternoon, to the Sandstone kennels, my conscience refused to allow me to simply "drop off" Kleenex, who was the victim of previously being "dropped off." I spoke with the Sandstone director about the possibility of Wally and me adopting her, because she would fit well with our current menagerie and have a loving, doting home with us. The director explained that the hour was late and we needed to follow protocol. I was instructed to return Kleenex to her kennel. Then I completed the required adoption paperwork which she signed and promised to leave it where the kennel manager would be sure to process it first thing in the morning. The director assured me that there would be no difficulty in our adopting Kleenex. The following morning, I arose very early to make the hour-and-a half drive to Sandstone. I arrived before their 8 a.m. opening; Kleenex had already been euthanized. "The kennel manager was just too busy to read the paperwork. These things happen." This half-baked explanation by the Sandstone director carried no apology, no sympathy.

Before I started to work very closely with humane associations and shelters in the state, I was under the naïve impression that because you chose to work with animals meant that you respected their life.

That tragic incident made me realize that in the future any dog I took with me to the schools would have to belong to Wally and me. But none of ours were disabled, and humane classroom lessons were more easily learned if my teaching dog had a handicap. I implored the two AHANM staff members who were responsible for the daily screening of all dogs to contact me when such a dog was chosen for euthanasia.

Sammy and I brought humane education to thousands of New Mexico classrooms.

The following week I received the phone call to come immediately to the clinic. A deaf dog was abandoned, brought to the shelter and scheduled that afternoon. I arrived within the hour and adopted Sammy, a long-haired blond Cocker Spaniel cross, painfully thin, with dull, sad brown eyes. After his exam and X-rays by the AHANM veterinarian, it was determined that Sammy was deaf, probably because he had been repeatedly hit or kicked in the head. His ribs had been broken and re-broken. There were internal injuries. Medicine and treatment were given and prescribed. His long tail wagging, our newest dog Sammy left AHANM with me to join our crew, "the guys."

By the end of 1999, *AHANM's* newsletter, *KindWords,* read: "**Forever X 13,000.** 'We will keep and love our pets forever,' was the response of the over 13,000 students and adults in 762 classrooms reached by educational volunteers for AHANM's *You and Your Pet Are Forever*."

Sammy's photo was big news in the newspapers of the schools we visited. It was a significant feather in our cap when his photo and our program made the front page of the February, 2000, issue of "*Perspective,*" an Albuquerque Public Schools newsletter, which served more than a hundred APS area schools.

Sammy's classroom experiences and friends made him famous and filled his life with a new experience: love. He was such a hit in the classrooms that students

Sammy is a star!

would send Christmas cards to AHANM addressed to "Sammy the education dog." Enclosed in most large envelopes were hand-decorated cards, along with a gift certificate for McDonald's french fries, Sammy's favorite after-school treat. Nor was his mail limited to the holiday season, as he received invitations to attend a variety of school functions throughout each year.

The home economics class in one mid-school on the east side of the state made him treats, shaped like a dog with very long ears. Another presented him with an assortment of sweaters, for his travels during the winter months. One student's hand-knitted sweater displayed the name and figure of the school's mascot, a large and ferocious bulldog. He drew many smiles when he sported that sweater.

During one of Sammy's and my earliest educational visit to Tome Elementary, located in a small community south of Albuquerque, I met the school librarian, Rebecca. She was a very special Houston lady with a winning smile and a heart the size of Texas. Because of her admiration for special-assistance dogs, she had driven to California to choose from those available by Canine Companions for Independence (CCI), a special puppy to temporarily foster and train. She and her new Labrador Retriever puppy, Orion, returned to Tome, where she assumed the strict guidelines as his "socializer" for the next twelve months.

Adhering to the training and guidance standards given her by the specialist staff at CCI, she assumed the duties as her dog's basic obedience-trainer. Identified by his brightly-colored green assistance vest, Orion was allowed to interact freely with the students of Tome Elementary. His status permitted him to visit all public places (schools, hospitals, businesses) so that he could experience situations he might later encounter as a working assistance dog. Rebecca was provided a list of specifics with which she was charged during Orion's very interesting and sometimes difficult puppy training.

The parent organization, CCI, provided a hotline and continual monitoring. It is accepted procedure that after the twelve to fourteen-month puppy training, the socializer would return the dog to the parent facility where his more intense and specific training would begin. Dogs in special assistance programs are trained, then tested in a particular category: mobility assistance, guide, walker, psychiatric, seizure alert/response, "Ssig" (sensory or social service) dogs and combo-dogs.

Before returning Orion to CCI, Rebecca gave him a farewell dinner party at one of the nicest area restaurants. I attended with Sammy, his Albuquerque bud. All of us were sad; some were tearful, but Rebecca was emotionally devastated. "I dreaded that this day would come," she lamented. "He has been my faithful companion, continually, twenty-four hours a day for the last

It's A Boy ! ! !

Name: Orion II
Date of Birth: February 22, 2002
Sire: Omsi/Quester   Dam: Abbey
Weight: 16 pounds
Date of arrival to New Mexico: April 24, 2002
Puppy Raiser: Rebecca Bootzin

Hello! My name is Orion. I am a golden retriever and labrador, and I am about 10 weeks old. As you can see from my photo, I am just precious. I am also a fast learner, and I will start puppy classes in a couple of weeks. I will live with Rebecca for about one year and learn basic commands and manners, then I will return to Canine Companions for Independence in California for advanced training. When I graduate from training school, I will become an assistance dog for a person in a wheelchair. My motto is: "Exceptional dogs for exceptional people."
I hope to see you soon !

Love,
Orion

twelve months. Orion has become such a part of me that I cannot bear to part with him, though I must honor my contract, my promise."

She and Orion spent a very quiet night with us to begin their return road trip to Santa Rosa, CA. There her sister from Texas met and consoled her, then the two drove back to Rebecca's new home with her sister, away from her Orion memories. I thought of her often during the coming months, of how difficult it is to emotionally recover, after relinquishing one's devoted pet.

But an unexpected and astonishing phone call would bring tears of joy for Rebecca and Orion's friends. "Kate, Wally, I am returning to California," she reported excitedly. "This time I am bringing Orion back to Houston with me. The school did not give a reason, but he did not pass his training. They offered me the opportunity to adopt him. I am elated. Orion and I will be, again, forever."

Her experience encapsulated the remarkable qualities of dogs. I am sure they were put on Earth by God to give us emotional and psychological strength, to teach us kindness, patience and responsibility, to save or better the lives of those in danger, to enrich the lives of those who are disabled, infirm or lonely, and to teach us love, for a dog is love.

In 2002 I left AHANM and began as education director for a no-kill shelter, Watermelon Mountain Ranch Animal Rescued (WMR), in Bernalillo, NM, a thirty-minute drive to the west of our home. The shelter volunteers were so enchanted by Sammy and his talents that his was the featured picture on their brochure and on my educational manuals, for which they underwrote the costs. The winter 2003 issue of Watermelon Melon Ranch publication *Ranch Roundup* featured Sammy's photo in their full-page article "*Humane Education Outreach Touches Children, Communities*." It was also featured prominently on their widely distributed brochure.

After six years, Sammy's health declined and he could no longer travel with me. A Rio Rancho school held a "retirement party" for Sammy. Gifts were abundant: stuffed toys and treats. His presence was greatly missed by both students and their teachers. Within four months, he was no longer able to even walk. I miss the determination, patience and strength of my well-loved and loving Sammy.

One of my dedicated and talented volunteer teachers, Linda Brady, rescued, during one of her training and fitness runs, a young, handsome black-and-white Parti Cocker

Brady's eyes were his ears.

Spaniel that had been tied to a piñon tree, abandoned in the Sandia Mountains. Because of her kindness, we named this sweet, deaf dog Brady, after Linda.

He was certified and ready to "wow" the classrooms within only a week. Brady did not prance, he danced. His unwavering eye contact with you was necessary for communication and made him easy to train. He was born for a life of showmanship.

After the "down" signal, he enjoyed performing a series of rolls and rolls and more rolls. Depending on the hand command, Brady shook hands with either paw and could bark or howl on command. He would crawl, changing directions at your pleasure. With prompting he could answer my questions with a nod in either direction. His ability to catch a variety of thrown objects—balls, Frisbees and toys—usually brought a "Standing O." What a guy!

These classroom antics and his popularity landed him, twice, the Watermelon Mountain Ranch trophy "For the Love of Children Pet of the Year." For many years, students from neighboring Rio Rancho, NM, would address their enthusiastic thank-you notes to "The Brady Bunch" at Watermelon Mountain Ranch Animal Rescue, Bernalillo, NM.

Until he was twelve, he continued to perform, ham it up and dances in hundreds of responsive classrooms across New Mexico.

These playful antics became history when, during a presentation to seventh grade prep-school students, a teenage girl crawled carefully and quietly under a nearby desk and fed him some unknown medications wrapped in cheese. Brady immediately went into seizures, frothing at the mouth.

We tried without success to locate the school nurse for hydrogen peroxide, which might have caused him to upchuck the pills. I was grateful that our veterinarian was close by. Abandoning my equipment and supplies, I scooped up Brady, who could no longer walk, and drove quickly to his office. His receptionist explained that because Brady did not have an appointment, even though he was in grave danger, Dr. Ridnoy would not see him.

Shocked at the indifference of her words, I explained further, "But Brady and our six other pets have been patients of Dr. Ridnoy for several years. This is an emergency."

"That is just my point," she replied tartly. "We do not see emergencies. Take him to an emergency clinic."

I turned to the two adult women waiting with their pets in his reception area and asked, "Would you please let me take Brady to see Dr. Ridnoy before your appointment? He is dying." Shocked at the situation, they nodded their agreement, but his receptionist would not allow it.

By the time we reached the emergency pet clinic several miles away, it was too late. My Brady's life could not be saved. Brady was one of many dogs I had lost since I was ten, because each ingested a dangerous substance, given to them by a mentally deranged individual. It was obvious that I should have taken more time with "poison-proofing" my dog: teaching your dog to never take food from someone's hand or pick up food from the ground without a release command of a chosen code-word. This is part of very basic lessons offered by most dog training centers. I had procrastinated that it wasn't important because I was always with my dogs, and—considering the number of dogs in our family—it would be too much of an undertaking. My carelessness in not "poison-proofing" Brady was partly responsible for his painful death.

Within its next two years, "*You And Your Pet Are Forever*" had reached over 35,000 students and teachers, in more than 2,000 classrooms, in eight New Mexico counties. When the time was included for scheduling, preparations, traveling and staff training, this volunteer education coordinator position had almost developed into a full time job. Its greatest benefit for me was to watch students change their attitudes about their responsibilities and their respect of their pets.

My most difficult classes were not to children but to the male members of the service organizations and clubs at which I spoke. Most were in total agreement that female dogs should be spayed. They were enthusiastic participants during the presentation…until I tried to convince these men to neuter their own male dogs. That was almost an impossible goal. It went against their macho posturing. They argued heatedly, even when I explained that once neutered, a male dog devotes less energy to the scents and dreams of those female dogs in heat that he can detect within a five-mile radius. That allows the neutered male dog more time to concentrate on the needs of his owner. The owner-bonding with a neutered male dog is now without competition, thus easier and faster.

I was also holding humane-education classes for interested animal educators throughout the state. One of those who attended a weekend class was Jeannie Cornelius. Since 1981 she had operated her animal rescue, Dixon Animal Protection Society (DAPS), about forty-four miles north of Santa Fe, NM. Serving an area that is underserved by local shelters, DAPS received most of their calls from the isolated areas in the mountainous areas of northern New Mexico. Its backbreaking chores and responsibilities take place daily because of the labors and donations of Jeannie, her husband, daughter and kind volunteers. Their only paid employees are an occasional local teen, on a special-need basis. Using donations and grant monies, they have cared for, housed, fed and placed hundreds of area abandoned dogs and cats. Her emergency program to help locally injured pets is offered by very few rescue organizations. It is always in demand and it is usually in red ink. Yet Jeannie and her family continue...for the love of animals.

I thoroughly enjoyed the challenge of my classroom activity in schools throughout the state. It was invigorating after a presentation to actually experience the effect of my instruction, the video, and student interactions. But I also felt impatience and disappointment that *"You And Your Pet Are Forever,"* then in its eighth year, had not had the immediate impact I had hoped. New Mexico's statistics for euthanasia and discarded pets still remained one of the highest in America.

One question from a twelve-year-old boy will always haunt me. He recounted to the fifth and sixth grade classes the story of his family dog, Sarge, who had grown old, and that his father decided, "Sarge has lived a long life with us, but now it is time for us to take him to the mesa."

The boy and his brother did not comprehend the significance of the trip to the mesa. When their dog did not return with their father, they really missed their friend Sarge. All through those summer months, they kept watching for him, before they realized that Sarge was not going to return. But early that winter, the family heard scratching on the back door, and opened it to find Sarge, excessively thin and filthy, but wagging his tail, happy to finally be reunited with his family. His father retrieved his rifle from the wall and without explanation, shot Sarge. The boy asked me, "Was my dad right to kill Sarge?"

Because this dramatic situation involved the attitude and action by a parent, it was not a question that an instructor could answer, so I asked the class to discuss this among themselves, then present and justify their opinions. With the exception of one student, they were unanimous in their verdict. The father's action had been cruel, violent and inhumane. Tears rolled down my face as these brave students, one after one, agreed with my heart. This was why I was teaching.

Clio was enjoying her peanutty dreams, 2002.

CHAPTER 15

CLIO'S CHALLENGE

"It's not the size of the dog in the fight;
it's the size of the fight in the dog."

– Mark Twain

Another physically impaired dog that served as my educator was Clio, a very small, twelve-pound, eighty-five-percent blind, brown-and-white Parti Cocker Spaniel, whose tenacity and superior attitude amazed our students. Born in 1998, Clio was a four-year-old owner-surrender, most likely from a backyard breeder in Albuquerque. She came with AKC registration (possibly the reason for her aloof attitude), which stated her name as Clio Althea Milo. All dog owners should be aware that AKC registration does not imply health or quality.

Watermelon Mountain Ranch Rescue, in their attempt to find her a loving home, featured this persnickety pup on television and in newspaper articles. She was even a featured guest of Lions Club and the Rotary in Rio Rancho. Sadly, no one wanted her and that included her current foster home.

Soon after adopting her from WMR in 2002, we had an appointment to visit a well-known eye surgeon, Dr. Roberts, for dogs in Loveland, CO., 500 miles north of Albuquerque. His patient explanation showed his deep respect for animals. His diagnosis was disappointing, "Surgery could have been a possibility earlier in her life. She is already four years old. I am sorry, but it is now too late for corrective surgery for her blindness."

Clio joined Brady in my travels and although they were an impaired pair, they were the perfect pair to demonstrate to the students how different the adjustments are that blind and deaf dogs are forced to make. In spite of their handicaps, their skills and sharp perception never ceased to bring "Ahhhhhhs" from the surprised classrooms.

Clio would perform almost any trick, complete with a

metronome tail, as long as the treat contained some form of peanut butter. To demonstrate how the acuity of other senses compensates for the loss of one, I would hide a tiny pouch with a spoonful of peanut butter in a spot chosen by each classroom. Little Clio would sniffing up and down the aisles, moving rapidly in her disco gait, swinging her bony backside to the

Clio: "Who cares if this hat covers my eyes?"

left while moving forward. Ignoring the mouth-watering temptations of open lunchpails and cookies on the desks, she would lead me straight to that hidden cache of her treasured peanut butter.

Although she was sightless, her Cocker Spaniel eyes continued to cause severe health problems for Clio. When she was eight, she was diagnosed with acute glaucoma in both eyes. This is a serious eye disease, in which fluid does not properly drain from the eye, causing the pressure inside the eye to increase. Not only is it very painful, but can also cause damage to the retina, optic nerve and other ocular tissues. In spite of medications, her disease progressed and Clio endured two ophthalmologic surgeries. Drains were inserted in her left eye to remove the buildup of fluid. A year later, her veterinarians were forced to remove her blind and painful right eye, a serious and involved surgical procedure termed enucleation.

To compensate for her lack of vision, she has depended on her remarkably extra-sharp sense of hearing and smell. Her ability to recognize even the softest sound was phenomenal. When we would carelessly fail to close and latch any door in our house, she was our only pooch to make a dash for that open door, regardless of where it led.

Clio's cutesy mannerisms made her appear to be exceptionally kissable, but she did not like to kiss or to be kissed. Kisses to any part of her curly head met with her "kiss-off," an immediate and violent shake-off of the "kiss-kooties." Only occasionally did she choose to be a lapdog, preferring to rest in her well-prepped, somewhat smelly though frequently laundered cushion. What a nester! Sometimes our cantankerous pup spent as long as five noisy minutes of concentrated energy "making" her bed or moving it away from our other dogs, whom, after eleven years she still refused to acknowledge.

Among our four dogs who were certified as therapy dogs, Clio was definitely the first choice of the residents in the retirement and nursing homes we visited. Possibly it was because she was so small and lightweight, which made her easier to hold for those with arthritis or in wheelchairs. Maybe she was so popular because she did not like to kiss. Many of the residents who had impaired vision found it difficult to see a kiss coming. At home, she was definitely not a "hold-me honey," but happily allowed the nursing home residents to cling to her for as long as they wished. Whatever, she was a tender part of their often tedious days. Residents wanted their photos (Wally was our official cameraman)

Clio was a favorite visitor at area retirement and nursing homes.

taken with her. Several even purchased peanut butter treats in anticipation of her next monthly visit, and in turn she brought them a freshly cut stem rose.

At fifteen she was totally blind and definitely hearing-impaired and no longer traveled to schools or nursing homes. She simply traveled around our yard, always with her own purpose. Clio was so fiercely determined that, once she honed in to her chosen site, she would shirk any directional guidance. Her acute sense of smell still enabled her to score at a peanut-butter hunt or make the open-door dash. On our annual Easter egg hunt on our patio, this elderly and blind dog bumped into and retrieved more eggs than any of our other six dogs, including our Retrievers.

When adopting a dog older than a year, all of us must accept that it comes with some behavioral quirks. Wally and I had never owned a more independent, less affectionate dog than Clio, and surmise that two events could have turned this energetic pup into such a loner: her blindness early in her life and the shock of being given away by a family whom she desperately loved. For years after we adopted her, we found her waiting by our front door, we thought waiting for her "real" (previous) owners to return. But visits to our home by a friend, Eddie, had always snapped her "to attention," with tail-wagging that seemed sonic-powered. And Eddie was showered with the kisses and loving that we have never received. Her reaction to his visits surprised us: Clio was actually capable of demonstrating affection. She was just waiting loyally for her original owners to return. How confused and heartbroken this blind little dog must have been when her family threw her away eleven years ago! Although we continually tried, we simply could not fill the place in her heart that her former owners held.

But the remarkable recovery made by this creature was admirable. Even her glaucoma and fairly recent deafness did not seem to faze this canine cutie as she continued, independently, at the same pace in her same routines. When confronted with physical ailments and emotional trauma, all of us could take lessons from this tenacious and stubborn creature, a definite survivor.

Babes, the national competitor, jumped with room to spare.

Chapter 16

WHAT A BABES!

"Babes is the best Pug ever to grace the jumps of agility."

**– Jane Winkler,
nationally recognized agility trainer**

143

A new rescue, a Pug, arrived in our lives in 1999 on a dark and rainy November night in a small town, Los Lunas, halfway between Albuquerque and Belen. The request came from Kelly Chapel, the hardworking and dedicated director of New Mexico Pug Rescue (NMPR). "Do you possibly have permanent room for one more rescue, an especially active, nine-month-old surrender?"

Originally named Angel, she and her owner moved from Iowa to Albuquerque when she was but a few months old. Her life changed drastically when her owner discovered that she herself was pregnant. Her superstitions held that you could not own a dog and be pregnant, so the owner delivered a less-than-six-month-old Angel to Animal Humane Association of New Mexico (AHANM) as an "owner surrender." Quickly adopted but just-as-quickly returned by her first adopting family, Angel, after a call from AHANM, became the ward of NMPR. Two other families who adopted this playful, perky puppy also found her irresistible, but voiced ridiculous reasons to return her to Kelly.

"She likes my husband better than me," was the pouty reason for her first return.

"She is much too lively, jumping all over the place," was the complaint of the second family.

Sadly, this was a three-strike situation, and although rescue groups try not euthanize, they must work quickly to find an appropriate owner when a dog has been returned by so many different, unhappy owners. In only three months, this small dog endured two separate shelters and four owners who found her "unsuitable." This lack of permanence can be so traumatic and confusing for the dog that it can greatly hamper its ability to become an adoptable, well-adjusted pet.

However, once we reached Los Lunas, this new Pug puppy was welcomed into open arms and broad shoulders. With his baseball background and its infield chatter (hom' babes), Wally named her Babes. Babes immediately adopted Wally, and on our return trip to Albuquerque from Los Lunas, could not be pried from his shoulders, where to this day, thirteen years later, she rests throughout Wally's reading of the morning paper and during his evening enjoyment of sports channels on TV. This new puppy would be our fourth Pug since we were married in 1962. Little did we know that she would become

Babes maintained her juxtaposition, on the right and behind.

our most talented, recognized, demanding, daring and dazzling, but also our most difficult Pug.

Kelly had described Babes as "high-spirited." What an understatement! Her actions on the next morning, her first day in our home, were a crystal ball as to what her future would hold. She greeted us holding her leash in her mouth. When we failed to respond appropriately, she dropped the leash and bolted for the goodie jar, where she performed her signature "twirl for treats." Indeed, Babes was a compact bundle of ceaseless kinetic forces.

She instantly turned our family room and kitchen into

an agility course: jumping from the couch to barstools to the countertop and down, onto chairs, through wrought iron dividers, down steps, over sleeping dogs, into trouble. All she wanted to do was run and jump, normal for most young dogs, but very abnormal for a Pug, whose internal dictionary does not process the word "athletic." Long and brisk walks were not the cure. Babes returned ready for more action. We learned to be also.

Eventually she would change most of our household routines to include her. Even my sweeping or mopping floors were no longer simple chores as she was determined to jump over the handles as they moved. This whirling dervish did not break stride all week. I was exhausted and our three other dogs were disgusted. Wally suggested that his dental hygienist, Jane Winkler, a nationally recognized and talented agility dog trainer, could help channel that energy. But before we approached Jane and asked for her help, we researched this canine sport we had only previously enjoyed watching on TV.

During agility competitions or trials, dogs of similar sizes compete with each other and against the clock while racing in a specific order in a set agility course. Their trainer's commands send them over or under hurdles, through tunnels, up and down steps, through weave poles.

But did Jane think that agility training might be the answer for Babes? Although she smirked at the idea of a Pug seriously performing the champion agility classes she taught, she suggested we first enroll Babes in puppy obedience classes, followed by novice advanced. Oh, Babes adored all the action and attention, but like all Pugs we had owned she was obstinate: her way or nothing at all. "Choice" was not in her vocabulary. Needless to say, her "Pug-tude" interfered with her obedience and agility training through-out that first year. But her sixteen-pound size, skills, speed and eagerness made it easier for the trainers to tolerate. It was no challenge for this headstrong, manipulative pup to "wrap" Wally and me for our evening training sessions. By the time Babes went into her routine, wagging that double-curled tail and squealing and jumping with excitement as our car approached her training site, she had easily melted our stern admonishments and commands down to a meek and ineffectual, "No, little Babes."

With ease, Babes worked the weaves.

At the end of the first year, having observed that Babes' possibilities were def-initely hampered by our pitiful techniques at training and dis-cipline, Jane politely suggested that dur-ing the coming year she should assume full responsibility for Babes' future training and traveling to AKC agility meets. We took the necessary photos and filed the required paper-work in order for Babes to be issued, by AKC, an Indefinite Privilege Listing Certificate allowing her to compete as a purebred Pug in AKC-sanctioned competitions. I jok-ingly interpret this pretentious IPL as her illegitimate Pug license.

Pugs are notoriously opportunistic, so Babes lost no

time winning Jane's heart and taking every possible advantage of her trainer's patience and talents. However, Jane's consistent coaching and intense determination of this thrown-away pug reaped awesome rewards during her very first national competition, September 2001, Denver, Colo. Babes won two novice titles, plus five blue and one red ribbon. By the end of that year, she earned a national Pug Dog Club Of America (PDCA) Agility number-five rating in Standard Courses. The following year, 2002, she earned the PDCA Agility number-one title, Jumpers with Weaves Courses and retained her 2001 title as number-five in Standard Courses. *Front and Finish*, November 2003, a dog trainer's publication, listed her as the number-one Agility Jumper Excellent Pug in 2002. AKC listed her as number-two Pug, nationally, in agility MACH (Master Agility Championship) competition.

*The Pug
Dog Club of America
cordially invites*

Babes AX AXJ

*To attend
"A Walk In The Park"
Top Twenty Conformation
And
Obedience & Agility
Showcase*

*Friday, October 3, 2003
8:30 P.M.
The Sturbridge Host Hotel
and Conference Center
Sturbridge, Massachusetts*

The next few years of training and travel paid off with a lion's share of titles, ribbons and publicity. One of her most touching moments of praise came from her trainer, Jane Winkler, who referred to her publicly as, "Babes, the best Pug ever to grace the jumps of agility." Competition became so intense that Jane even requested that Wally and I not attend her meets, as our presence seemed to affect, in a negative way, Babes' performance on the agility courses.

*Jane Winkler was not only Babes' talented trainer,
but also her most supportive fan.*

Because of her professional training by Jane, Babes was also honored by being inducted into the PDCA Top Twenty Conformation and Obedience and Agility Showcase in an October 2003 celebration in Sturbridge, MA.

Wally made sure that few visitors to our home were spared the visit to "The Babes' Hall of Fame." On numerous shelves in our family-room bookcase are showcased her recognized feats of agility. Around framed award photos, patches, plaques, statues and certificates flowed a multitude of ribbons of varying colors and sizes, designating meet location, event time and earned place and title patches, certificates.

While giving them this "Babes Tour," Wally jested that he had once hoped, while in high school or college, that his baseball and basketball skills might land his name or picture in a national sports magazine. He had to settle, instead, for

*Wally was proud of his Babes, a discarded Pug,
who climbed to #1 Pug in agility.*

his photo in the March 2002 issue of *"Pug Talk,"* capturing Babes in her most comfortable position, on his shoulder, just as she sat that rainy night in 1999 when we adopted her from NMPR in Los Lunas.

Sadly, her 2006 annual visit to the veterinarian revealed heavy deposits of calcium on her vertebrae, cause for occasional pain and definitely cause to remove Babes from the agility circuit. Kurt still called her "Babes-a-rific," his term of endearment to describe her outstanding athletic abilities, agility ratings and her above-it-all behavior.

She still was the star in our household as well as in the annual fund-raising summer "Pugnics" and autumn "Pugtoberfests," co-sponsored by New Mexico Pug Rescue and Bow Wow Blues in Albuquerque, an unusual and upscale pet accessory store, whose grassed back yard was boneshaped. Always a competitor, Babes' agility skills at their

*Pug Light Beer and Babes Ruth
were winners at annual Pugnics.*

cheeseball toss and bobbing for hotdogs gave her the edge. Her homemade costumes portraying PugLite Beer, Blue Ribbon Babes, Lady Pug, Babes Ruth, Pugskin and the infamous "Runaway Bride" were prizewinners, too.

These Pug-family gatherings always buzzed with infectious laughter as more than 100 Pugs and their permissive and doting owners let down their hair and participated in other imaginative and ludicrous competitions such as Pug and parent look-alikes, best kissers, trick-or-treat games, curliest tails or most wrinkles. I've often thought that since deep facial wrinkles are a physical trait of all Pugs, the Pug winning the most wrinkles covering its smooshed-in face would make a hilarious subject for anti-aging creams for a television commercial.

Always a competitor, Babes still held onto one title: the title to manipulate, maneuver and pout. You would never

Babes entertained all ages.

use the word "sweet" to describe her personality. Because she had never been under the false impression that all dogs are created equal, she had no qualms about pushing the other dogs around, especially one of our apprehensive cockers, a compliant Scamper.

Her need to dominate began early each morning. Worse than the crowing of any early-morning rooster, Babes, in drill sergeant fashion, barked off her vocal instructions regarding promptness and amounts of breakfast food. It was hysterical when she actually levitated with dissatisfaction.

She expected her role as boss to be respected all day long. When one of our other unassuming dogs, for whatever reason, displeased her, this eighteen-pound stick of dynamite ambled over to the dog, and regardless of its size, Babes gave it "the hip," which was our term for a quick jab of her hip against the dog's leg, her sign of ultimate disapproval. The fact that this overt action was usually ignored by the other dogs just incensed her to resort to barking

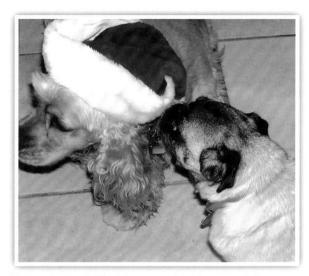

Babes barked Christmas orders to sweet Scamper.

verbal reprimands, also dismissed as ludicrous. When Wally observed her display of aggravating and anti-social behavior, he would calmly walk over, gently pick Babes up, give her a soft reprimand, and place her on his lap while he finished reading.

She displayed the perfect selfish and vain personality to be correctly cast as "*Miss Piggy,*" the capricious central character of *The Muppet Show*, a very popular TV series. The physical resemblance was strong too. This dictatorial little Pug actually snubbed us for at least a day after our return from a vacation. She accomplished this obnoxious behavior by promptly leaving any room we entered and by not sounding-off her early-morning feeding orders. (We suffered that easily by sleeping later.)

Juxtaposition rules. According to the "Book of Babes," her rightful position was always on or next-to Wally (on the right side only). After meals she insisted that she occupy Wally's lap as he sat at the breakfast-room table, thus assuring her greater access to possible leftovers. During the day she perched on the highest area of the couch, giving her, she felt, total safety and a broader view, thus more power. Her possessiveness got the best of her if Wally, not only allowed on his right side, but also petted another of "the guys" while relaxing on our "quilted couch" (a hodge-podge of irregular-sized, brown leather patches varying in textures and shades, glued to cover the numerous taste tests taken by each new puppy we have adopted over the years). Babes would then refuse to sit near Wally, moving to the farthest corner of the couch while staring daggers at him until he moved the offending, unaware and unselfish pet to the other, left side of his legs.

If she was not resting on, above or (on the right side) next to Wally, she staked out her territory on the rug below the goodie jar, just in case. Since her arthritis no longer allowed her to do her daily twirl for treats, it is important she made "first claim." Location is everything. What a supercilious, spoiled dog! What a Babes!

Babes entertained Wally's mother while she
oversaw the preparation of her breakfast.

Our sweet Scamper was on the scent, 2009.

CHAPTER 17

SIMPLY SCAMPER

"The weak, the lame, the infirm are our strongest reason to look inward for the strength to make a difference."

– Eileen Jacobson

One April 2002 evening at a Watermelon Mountain Ranch Animal Rescue (WMR) staff gathering, the co-owner and founder, Sophia, directed me to a kennel that her husband, Lee, had just unloaded from the rescue's beige SUV. Whining in a rear corner of the kennel and trembling so badly as to rattle the kennel, was a very young, blond Cocker Spaniel-cross, with some of the largest, most longing eyes I had ever seen. He also had, from his nose to his closely cropped tail, the largest number of puffed-up, engorged gray dog-ticks I had ever seen on any canine. (I call them Stephen King Ticks because their vulgar appearance evokes horror.) In response to a call from a concerned motorist, Lee had picked him up at the crossing of two state highways, 550 in Bernalillo and 528 in Rio Rancho, NM, which shares its southern boundary with Albuquerque.

Sophia asked, "Once Watermelon takes this terrified pup to our veterinarian for exam, inoculations, and de-ticking, would you foster him? He needs to be much less fearful and build some confidence before he can be presented for adoption."

Fortunately, Wally and I seemed to have a calming effect with excessively frightened animals (and we were also easy marks). When we looked at this poor frightened, cowering animal, there was no other choice. We agreed to her request.

Only six days later Sophia called us to pick up her new rescue, our new foster. But when we arrived, we realized that he was still covered with these fat, gray ticks. His long blond locks had been shaven in an attempt to locate and remove the multitude of these repulsive arachnids that covered his small, slender body. She explained that the veterinarian had put him in an insecticidal de-ticking solution, but because it was so potent, the dog could not be immersed again for another two weeks. In the meantime, several of the more tenacious ticks remained.

Both Wally and I were concerned because we had at home six other dogs for which we were responsible. We would volunteer to foster him only after he had no remaining ticks. Almost three weeks later Sophia again brought the puppy to our home, proclaiming that, this time, he was indeed "tick-free."

Wrong!!!! The next morning, we found three gray gorged ticks crawling on the utility room floor. Thank goodness that a hasty but thorough exam found that none of these blood-sucking insects had yet to infect any of our six dogs, but our new boarder certainly needed further treatment. Our patient and understanding veterinarian was able to work us in for an emergency appointment that morning. This poor frightened puppy (we called him Scamper) still had a large infestation of ticks. After receiving instruction on how to handle this ugly problem at home, we made a temporary, comfortable home for Scamp in a nearby small, seldom-used room, placing rolled towels around the door to prevent the escape of these disgusting ticks. Next, twice daily, Wally and I intrepidly tackled our charge, our offensive duty, with a bottle of alcohol, a pair of tweezers, and steady hands, removing both head and mouth parts of each attacking parasite we found. These procedures took nine days before our veterinarian assured us that our long-suffering, stressed-out Scamper was tick-free...and free, finally to socialize and meet our other guys.

He was, of course, shy and standoffish, frightened and

distrustful, choosing the wallflower approach of remaining in the corner of the room, alone on his cushion, displaying not the slightest desire of becoming friends with the other dogs or even with us. Only after he became uncontrollably hungry or otherwise in need, would he leave the safety of his cushion for food or water or a relief trip outside. This sad behavior lasted for several months, until finally he would allow only me to go near him. And Wally and I thought that there was another handicap working against his adjustment, as there were several instances in which we doubted the acuity of Scamper's eyesight.

The cards were stacked against his being adoptable. Although Wally and I had tried, Scamper was still a long way from being ready to meet the public. Watermelon realized that his apprehensive demeanor was that of a severely abused dog, and this was working against his being adoptable. When that decision was made, of course, Scamper became a permanent one of "the guys."

After six years of gentle coaxing and tempting with an assortment of treats and toys, Scamper finally had a brave moment and jumped up on the sofa next to Wally for pets and praise. What a surprise! What a memorable, tearful occasion! Now they were "almost buds."

But our sweet Scamper was still tortured by every new individual or situation he encountered. He was not a wimp, just painfully uncertain. The only action he displayed that was the least bit aggressive was to bark and howl uncontrollably, ceaselessly when he was in the back yard. No person, pet, noise or movement motivated or set in motion this compulsive behavior, for which no yet-published solution worked. We would consider it to be a comical form of

*Our shy Scamper waits patiently with "the guys"
as their Great Room is being spruced-up.*

bravery if it wouldn't be so annoying to our neighbors, and justifiably so. But he was a champ, expecting and accepting his necessary muzzle when he was in the yard, and his diaper when he came inside.

ASPCA (American Society for the Prevention of Cruelty to Animals) recently opened its Behavioral Rehabilitation Center in Madison, NJ, to address such extreme apprehension in dogs, usually the result of animal cruelty. Previously this chore was the responsibility of shelters, that if unsuccessful were forced to euthanize these frightened animals. Because this two-year project will only be able to work with about 400 dogs, there will be no immediate relief for shelters. However, if successful, this research could have a widespread impact on all abused pets and their new, adopted and puzzled owners.

Scamper was as handsome as he was sweet.

Scamper appeared to have had an Afghan as a distant cousin. Coupled with his mostly Cocker appearance, this genetic makeup made him one of the most handsome dogs we had ever seen, with his long cream, tri-colored wavy fur, his amazingly large and tender brown eyes and long lush eyelashes to die-for.

Daily he assumed his position as sentry on a black leather chair facing our north back yard. He entered his "special place" and became unmovable, unresponsive, impervious

Scamper slumbers during sentry duty.

to his surroundings, seemingly entranced by what he was observing. Unfortunately, Scamper had trouble learning almost everything. This was another reason that ten years ago, Watermelon could never find a good, loving home to accept him. Tests by our veterinarian on Scamper did not reveal either faulty hearing or eyesight. Behavioralists and veterinarians he visited attributed this to an unknown trauma before he was rescued or possibly he was born just the way he was—simply unaware, simply Scamper.

Surprisingly, he was our only dog who seemed to care about the hard knocks taken in the daily life of our sightless Clio. When he was nearby and could tell that Clio was going to hit an immovable object head-on, Scamper would quickly put himself between Clio and that projecting wall, fence, table, chair or whatever was in her path. He may have been short on smarts, but he was certainly long on caring.

All of God's creatures have frailties. We loved him deeply, and were humbled when he was able to display any affection toward either of us that was not associated with food or a goodie. We were satisfied that, occasionally, sweet Scamper felt that we, Wally and I, his master and mistress, were among those goodies in his simple life.

Our annual Easter egg hunt was rewarding for both Scamper and Ella.

Peaches, despite her blindness, pranced to a different drummer.

CHAPTER 18

BFF–If

"It only takes one person to throw an animal away,
but it takes a whole team to find him a home."

– **Unknown**

The following year in April 2003, I was volunteering at the Watermelon Ranch Spring Adopt-a-Thon, held on the New Mexico State Fairgrounds. This was always a hectic and a happy weekend event, bringing together prospective dog owners with their newly chosen pets. Our many people-friendly dogs and puppies, cats and kittens were placed in an assortment of kennels, in shaded areas. Volunteers were on duty and on alert so that no over-friendly children or adventurous adults put their fingers or something harmful into the kennels. We were present to answer questions, remove a pet from its kennel for any interested individual or family, and service the pets' needs by adding water to their bowls and removing waste. Some just needed a calming pet or a few softly spoken words, as this was such a different environment for them.

While we were busy directing, diverting and disposing, the administration was registering interested adults, reviewing their required paperwork and approving and recommending pets for new homes. Adopt-a-Thons, known by an assortment of names throughout different communities, are actually the recycling of thrown-away pets into new households eager for the special devotion and companionship that only pets can give, a love with no strings attached.

Quite a commotion caused me to look up from filling water bowls. Slowing making their way toward our main enclosure were a mother and her teenage daughter, pulling a small strawberry-blonde Cocker Spaniel puppy with a big, heavy chain leash. It was an ugly scene. They were continually hitting the puppy with the chain, and each time one of them hit the already bloodied puppy with the sizable metal chain, the dog would retaliate by lunging and growling at them. They were oblivious to their sickening display of wanton cruelty in public, a public that had gathered and watched in horror.

"All we want to do is to get rid of this damn dog, now. Take her. Peaches is nothing but trouble," the mother complained. As if this were some inanimate object she had been thrashing, the mother then threw the chain at the dog. Seemingly relieved and without a care, these two deranged women stomped away and departed the fairgrounds, leaving this badly injured and traumatized, cowering pup bleeding in the soil, still striking out viciously at all around her. We were all so shocked with this horrific display of violence that none of us had even thought to stop them or to have them complete the owner-surrender forms. We had absolutely no information about the mother and daughter so we could report their reprehensible behavior to City Animal Services. It had caught us totally off-guard. No one had even alerted fairground security.

Watermelon's owner-director, Sophia, her husband, Lee, and their animal handler, Robert, each cautiously and repeatedly approached this frightened Cocker, but she was terrified and in pain, striking out furiously, lunging and growling at anyone nearby.

What did this poor dog know of the intent of these strangers? We had just witnessed that her past experience with her humans led to severe pain and the need to defend herself.

Their reaction and responsibility was one of safety: call City Animal Services because this dog was not only aggressive and dangerous but also injured. While we waited for animal services to respond, I had an idea. *Why not? I have nothing to lose, but this little dog does.*

Hot dogs to the rescue! Because of today's Adopt-a-Thon, they were ready, bagged in my pocket, sliced, moist, greasy and warm. Cautiously, I placed them on the ground between the frenzied Cocker and the place where I would sit. Tossing a bunch in her direction, for scent and taste, I then sat on the ground and waited. Robert opened a few wire kennels and placed them in a circle around me, so that the public would be safe and the frightened dog could not get away. It took her about twenty minutes to calm down enough to take notice of the treats. Amazing! One by one she gobbled them up. She followed my hot dog trail to where I was sitting, and without hesitation, she jumped on my lap and finished devouring the hot dogs that I still had in my hand. She remained on my lap, and returned home with me permanently.

But on the way home, it was necessary that our veterinarian take several stitches in a muzzled, very strong, apprehensive and angry puppy. Two months later she was well enough to spay and inoculate. Hot dogs, of course, were and have been since, her reward for good behavior.

Although we kept her name, Peaches, I affectionately called her BFF–if (Best Friends Forever—if I had hot dogs). For the safety of all, it was necessary that we boarded her in a room separated from our other dogs. Her adaptation to our home was slow and laborious. It took Wally and me several months of very quick hands and slow, cautious behavior to avoid getting bitten ourselves, as Peaches was still distrustful, frightened and in some pain.

In her beginning years, Peaches' severe apprehension and tendency to nip when frightened, excited or touched made her undesirable for adoption or for appearing with my classroom presentations of *"You and Your Pet Are Forever."* For years, she would yelp, as if in pain, when a stranger touched her sides. But she successfully found her niche with "the guys" as yet another pretty but pushy broad.

It was quite some time before we felt Peaches was safe around other people, and before we could assume the role of responsible pet owners, and enroll her in obedience training. She was so quick to learn that the astonished instructor issued her training certificate after only the first week of a six-week class. As always hot dogs helped. However, when we returned home on that Friday afternoon, we released her in the back yard to play where, for the next thirty minutes, she blithely ignored our commands, "Come, Peaches! Peaches, come!" This situation was both maddening and ludicrous. Was this the same dog that had just been prematurely awarded her Novice Obedience Certificate? Her overdose of free will could be troublesome.

For the next almost ten years Peaches became fearless of everything except people. She was a whirling dervish, reconnoitering and investigating during all of her waking hours. Peaches continued to search on the trail of trouble, almost totally oblivious to presence of our other "guys" as well as to the calls of her permissive owners. This curiosity along with her super-strong senses of hearing, sight and smell kept her much too busy to nap or to lap like the rest of "the guys." Instead her small, firm but fully packed and muscular body was in a constant state of investigative work checking the many wildlife scents in our large back yard with naturally-occurring native shrubs, trees and a small underground stream. When the current trail became cold, Peaches would take a break, for only a short period of time, to play with us, her tail a metronome, ready for a tummy rub or a slobbery tennis ball game, with which she quickly became bored. Wally attributed this to my coordination, or lack of, citing, "You throw like a girl."

Peaches had never socialized indoors with any of our other dogs except Brady. After his death, she found a new friend, not an indoor but an outdoor friend, a silly squirrel. Several times a week for years, this squirrel or some squirrel (they all look alike) traveled to our courtyard so she and Peaches could go through an identical routine on each visit. This squirrel did not perform for our other guys, only Peaches. Peaches waited patiently each morning by the breakfast-room glass door for the visit of her friend, Squirrelly, who scampered from an evergreen limb, jumped down next to the door, and wagged its big, long furry tail against the glass, where Peaches was waiting. She, of course, went ballistic, barking loudly, but Squirrelly was not intimidated, did not budge, and continued wagging its tail. This tease was repeated a couple of times each week.

Peaches found great pleasure in her other friends, a collection of small, soft, stuffed animals that made a variety of sounds. They rested, with her, on her cushion in the utility room, Peachie's Place, where she actually petted them. They were never gnarled; the seams of these special friends were intact for years, and as long as I kept the batteries changed, their safely hidden soundboxes still recited childhood nursery rhymes, and "moos" or "meows." Her attachment to her stuffy friends made Peaches, once more, an easy target for teasing, to the utter delight of our Golden Retriever, Rex and Kurt's Labrador, Ella, who continually stole and hid her stuffy friends.

Peachy: "I could be Santa's BFF… if he has hot dogs."

Only three weeks short of her tenth birthday, her Cocker genetics threw her a low blow. We noticed that her right eye was inflamed and weeping. Our concerned veterinarian worked us in immediately, but it was inevitable. Glaucoma coupled with Sudden Acquired Retinal Degeneration (SARD) would permanently claim, within two months, her vision in both eyes and her sense of smell. For SARD there is no known treatment.

In our past experiences, we had found that eye medications were usually very difficult to administer, regardless of the treat, to our more active dogs. However, our uneasy and fidgety BFF—if actually tolerated sitting quietly for her morning and evening eyedrops, if… her bravery was rewarded with hot dogs. She was a firm believer in, "A good dog is a goodie-trained dog."

*Peaches presented an example of how mischief
can be wrapped in an adorable package.*

We were saddened when, after four months, the prescribed eyedrops could no longer help her glaucoma. Her eye pressure became painful, and additional treatment had to be chosen. While Peaches was briefly under anesthesia, intravitreal injections were made into both eyes by her ophthalmology-certified veterinarian. While recovering, we successfully spoiled her even more by allowing her extra naps in "people beds" and lots of other "Peachie-perks."

Confused by her sudden but permanent blindness and loss of smell, she countered with several defense mechanisms. If her acute hearing picked up any sound that she could not identify, she began to bark uncontrollably. She was not comfortable being in the yard without one of us, and barked frantically if she thought we had left her alone. Because she could no longer be the Willie Mays of our dog world, she lacked interest in any games. It was understandable that Peaches' adjustments would take time, requiring that we continually worked together on routines to make her life easier and ours less noisy. Although, in the past, Beulah, Alice, Rusty, Muffin and Clio had all experienced blindness during their lives, we were not aware of the websites blinddogs.com, fetchease.com, handicappedpet.net, deafdogsforever.weebly.com. They provided incredible support, sensible ideas and even a few games with rolling noise toys or beeping toys which Peaches did learn to enjoy.

The population of congenitally deaf, blind or deaf/blind canines are increasing in our shelters and humane rescue organizations. Blind dogs are estimated at 300,000. Although no data exists regarding possible behavioral issues in blind dogs, Strain and some AKC breed groups advocate their euthanasia at birth.

Our experience with these dogs, mostly rescues of course, has shown that they are no more prone to aggression or other behavioral disorders than other dogs we have owned or rescued. Our combined sixty years of experiences actually revealed that our eight blind or deaf dogs were easier to train. With the exception of Clio, they even bonded more quickly with us, their new owners.

Illinois State University has launched a Canine Behavior Laboratory to provide a means of behavioral rehabilitation for foster and rescue dogs, who are now housed in campus facilities. One student noted that working with blind or deaf dogs has taught the participants not to form prejudicial thoughts and that this gem of learning should be carried over when one assesses peers who suffer impairments.

Various studies of blind canines are continuing and most

address, in great depth, the newly adjusting dog's dependency on their owner.

And inside or out, our Peaches compensated by shadowing me as close as the situation would allow. Her new walk was slow, low to the ground, crouched in a predator-like posture. Thankfully, we were introduced to a new and innovative leash for blind dogs, which we kept clipped to Peaches' collar at all times, and it worked fairly well. Thin and stiff, with its tubular cord enclosed in leather, these leashes were designed to give dogs a much stronger sense of being safely led. Expert lessons on training a blind dog can be found on the DVD or VHS forty-eight minute, award-winning film *New Skills For Blind Dogs* by Landmark Publication Studios.

Despite her blindness, Peaches still pranced to a different drummer. More so than ever, it was *my* responsibility, to remain *her* BFF, to be there to help and guide her with her sudden loss of vision. She was my BFF, no "if" about it.

Delilah came to us with a heavy heart.

CHAPTER 19

SWEET DREAMS, DELILAH

"A trained dog is a happy home."

In 2007 it was necessary for me to leave my volunteer position at Watermelon Mountain Ranch to fill in for my husband's dental assistant-receptionist, Lela, who had decided to retire. Lela certainly earned that retirement, as she began her dental career with Wally forty years earlier, in 1967, at Hope Medical Center in Estancia, NM, when she was only seventeen years old. She was such a loyal, loving and trustworthy individual that we have always, with great pride, considered her to be our adopted daughter. Because she was quick to share freezer-burn meat and fish from her overstocked freezer with our dogs, Lela's generosity represented a series of many special meals to "the guys."

Wally retired the following year, October 2008, sold his dental practice, and we both looked forward to enjoying the fruits of retirement. With additional and unscheduled time in our lives, we could now rescue more unwanted dogs and could pursue stronger legislation to protect New Mexico's animals.

In January 2009, nine weeks into retirement, I answered a phone call that would sadden and drastically alter our lives. I did not recognize the caller's voice, and the caller ID, a New Mexico area code, gave me no clue.

"I'm sorry that your daughter died such a tragic death. She was beautiful and a good friend." Silence.

I was shocked, speechless, tongue-tied. More silence. *What did he say?* Minutes went by without a sound. Ahhhh, hello, who is this?"

"Have you found her will yet? I'm to be the executor, you know?" the male voice continued.

My reaction was to hang up this offending phone, which I managed, unsteadily but softly, then tearfully found

Wally. I was trembling and confused. We hoped this was a sick crank call from someone mentally deranged. We had the number stored on our phone. *Should Wally call and confront the unidentified caller?*

Our phone rang again within the next thirty minutes, same phone number. This time it was Wally who picked up the receiver. "Dr., you remember me, Hernando Sena. My mother and I were patients of yours. I wanted to give you and your wife my heartfelt condolences on your daughter's recent, untimely and ugly death. I was there with her, you know, when she finally died," he chatted on as if this were a social call. "Have you made arrangements? Have you found her will? I deserve to know. It lists me as her executor."

Trying to get his thoughts together and remain calm, Wally hesitated, then asked, "Where is she, Hernando?" Our caller hung up.

Sadly, we had not heard from our only daughter, Miss Kate, now forty-one, in several years. She had no telephone land-line and changed cell-phone numbers, all unlisted, like most people change linens, so we had no current number to call. Her nomadic acquaintances in the area had no current phone numbers listed. Fortunately we had visited her Santa Fe home, so we had that address. Fruitless, frantic and tearful hours were spent calling the Santa Fe City Police Department, then the Santa Fe County jail and finally the morgue located in St. Vincent Hospital. Their helpful and sympathetic employees found no records, no one answering her description, etc...thank goodness! And thank goodness, no more frightening Hernando calls.

But at eleven that evening, we did receive a solemn call, followed by a home visit from the Santa Fe Sheriff's

Department confirming our fears. Because of our calls to the Santa Fe Police Department, they had alerted the sheriff because her residence was in the county. Two deputies had discovered her body, in her home, where her yellow Labrador Retriever fiercely had stood guard for several days. Santa Fe Animal Shelter and Humane Society (SFAS&HS) had been radioed to pick up her dog and four cats, all of whom were rescue animals, as Miss Kate, too, was an animal lover.

By the time we drove sixty miles to Santa Fe, inspected and secured her home, we were devastated, confused, exhausted and overcome with grief. Understanding our situation and our depressed state of mind, the shelter director had kindly volunteered to wait for us, even though it was late and after-hours. And we were pleasantly surprised when this kind man drove to meet us because we had lost our way to their newly built shelter. What dedication and kindness!

The compassion with which they handled this tender transaction was impressive. When a pet owner dies, the policies of the Santa Fe Animal Shelter dictated that they examine, bathe and inoculate, if necessary, each intake animal at no charge to a new owner. The three-day stay of Miss Kate's five pets was also without fee, in respect of the grave situation. SFAS&HS was to be commended for enforcing such a generous and humane policy. To show our appreciation, not only did we, but also our friends and family, made annual donations in Miss Kate's memory to this special shelter.

We had brought kitty kennels from home (Oh, yes, we had always been home to a cat or two also.) Even in our spacious Camry, it took talent to load and stabilize four hard, formed kennels on our back seat so that they wouldn't slide, and still leave room in the back for Miss Kate's sizable Labrador. Kurt, Wally and I planned to squeeze into the front seat for the drive back to Albuquerque.

But we had grossly miscalculated the size of her over-weight Lab, Delilah. She not only couldn't fit in the allotted space in the back seat, but was also determined to sit next to Wally, the driver, in the front. I was left with no other choice than to take Delilah's allotted place in the back, next to the kitties. It was a long, odorous but eerily quiet hour and a half before we finally reached home that evening. We were moving slowly, still in shock. It would be several hours later before we had Kate's cats comfortably settled in a room by themselves and Delilah successfully introduced to our five dogs: Babes, Clio, Ella, Peaches and Scamper.

After a week of dragging around the house, probably searching for her beloved Miss Kate, Delilah laboriously jumped onto the couch next to Wally, to announce that she was officially ours. We began her twice-daily walks around the neighborhood, and, in absence of snacks, tried to spoil her with praise and affection. She lapped it up.

She studied our laid-back pet scenario. Dogs were resting on cushions thrown all over the floors. Dogs were sprawled on both black leather chairs and on her brown leather couch. Dog toys, too, were scattered around the rooms. Dog treats were handed out for just a bit of begging. Without further observation, she knew we were "easy pickins."

The shyness disappeared. Delilah's hidden personality emerged. She wasted no time in assuming the "alpha" role, much to the chagrin of Babes, who thought her bossiness

In disbelief, Delilah asked Babes, "You are alpha, really?"

constituted being boss, top dog. Because the "other guys" could care less, her new role was accepted without incident, only grumblings from Babes.

Delilah had decided that because she wanted to, she would sleep with me downstairs, where I was recovering from recent rotator-cuff surgery. She would dash eagerly each day at 1 and 8 p.m., to my temporary bedroom and wait impatiently for me to follow, wagging her tail and dramatizing the "Sad Eyes Dog Ploy-Number Five" until I opened the bedroom door. The king-sized mattress was rather high, so we thoughtfully purchased a large doggie stepstool. With her sizable head resting near my pillow, I kissed her wet nose and wished her, "Sweet dreams, Delilah."

So, what's your next trick, Frankenstein?

Our veterinarian had calculated the weight that eight-year old Delilah needed to lose, for health reasons, was twenty pounds and prescribed a strict feeding regimen. As a result, both immediately following and in-between her two daily meals, she moped near the food bin, anticipating, hoping. *Couldn't we see hunger in her sad eyes?*

Surprise! Delilah-of-Many-Talents could use her large sweeping tail to remove leftovers from the breakfast-room table, which certainly gave her an assortment of ill-gotten edibles to offset the restricted morsels she was being fed while on her diet.

She wasn't sharing, so Peaches blew the whistle. Her shrill barking called our attention to our enterprising Lab. The result was a more punctual and responsible clearing of our dishes.

Once she discovered our two apple trees that summer, we nicknamed her Eve. She could not resist those apples, despite their squishy, past-maturity form, and was consuming them at an incredible rate. This was not "an apple a day" healthy habit. We were forced to fence a new section, on

"Look into my hungry eyes," Delilah begged.

the north of our already fenced-in yard, away from the apple trees, for her to roam. Those fallen apples, though raked twice daily, were also a temptation to the bears, posing a different, more serious danger. It took more than a year, but she slowly lost her excess pounds, developed a healthy coat and a spry step, making it more difficult to keep up with her during our early morning walks.

Each of us fell immediately for this loveable Lab. She pulled you right in with those pleading eyes, that sweet disposition and what you thought was her need to please you. Of all of our wonderful, loving pets, she was our sweetest, our most adorable, our easiest to adore. She was number one among equals, coyly "calling the shots" even when we were not aware of it.

My words cannot explain the hole in our hearts, the void in our lives that her death from cancer left. *We miss you. Sweet dreams, our darling Delilah.*

Smoky and Patches brought an automatic smile to Kurt's face.

CHAPTER 20

OUR DOG HOUSE
ALLOWED CATS

"One small cat changes coming home to an empty house to coming home."

– Pam Brown

You have surmised that it is with great difficulty and determination that we had also been able to house cats, whom we admired and adored, in the very same home as our dogs (whose numbers varied from four to eleven). Consider that at any given time, one or more of our dogs might not be a "cat" dog, and one or more of our cats might not be a "dog" cat. Because both species were our responsibility and we could not take any chances, our felines and canines could not reside in the same area. Applying our imagination to a well-designed floor plan, we had been able to make our current lodging arrangements pet-friendly since 1976, our first year in this spacious home.

When we returned from the Santa Fe Animal Shelter and Humane Society with Miss Kate's four frightened kitties, we placed them together in a roomy, downstairs, screened-in porch, ten feet by twenty-eight feet. From Animal Humane in Albuquerque, we purchased a perch, a scratching post, some beds, bowls, litter boxes and toys. Our only cat at the time, an indulged Miss-ter Kitty, had shared our upstairs bedroom for many years, and would not have welcomed any interloper.

We were having a difficult time finding loving and stable homes for her cats. This was early 2009, the second year in a row to set records for real estate foreclosures. Job losses and abysmal economic conditions were making mincemeat of the finances of many of Miss Kate's friends, making their lives too uncertain and their monetary situation too shaky to assume the responsibility of a new pet. We acted cautiously and placed only two, Tiger and Puff, with couples we hoped had a sound financial future. We kept Pudgie and his girlfriend, Oreo Cookie, both seemingly inseparable and both had previously stayed with us for many months.

Pudgie was appropriately named by Miss Kate. He was seriously overweight (sixteen pounds) but a handsome and gentle kitty. Approximately fourteen years old, he was the sweetest, most affectionate and friendly cat we have ever had. That was a bold statement, as all of our cats except Panther have been sugar-sweet and purr-fectly friendly. Once we put him on a strict diet, his body assumed its natural form and the swirling pattern of his tricolor dark gray, black-and-white fur took on a unique marbleized appearance.

Cancer claimed this fantastic feline three years later, in the summer of 2012. Wally, Kurt and I felt a terrible void, along with Oreo Cookie, who for her entire eleven-year life, had been Pudgie's girl and was now alone.

Oreo Cookie was a ten-year-old, extremely small (five pounds) and dainty cat whose very long black fur made her appear much larger and heavier. Miss Kate also named her aptly because her black lips had an uneven smear of white fur with a small white drip on her nose. Of course she wore a white bib, a complement to her stark black and beautiful appearance. Sweet, shy and soft are all descriptive adjectives that suited this very vocal and loving kitty who craved continual cuddling and petting.

We wished she could have lived with our present upstairs mate, Miss-ter Kitty, an Abyssinian cross, who was rescued in 2005 by Kurt from an apartment house, where he had been dumped by moving tenants, cruel and indifferent. Kurt thought that this tiny abandoned kitty could get some good loving from us and vice versa. We were hooked at the first "meow" and took this new black-and-gray peppered-patterned kitten to our vet for inoculations, spaying, and an initial exam. So skinny, to the point of being emaciated, we named her Miss Twiggy, after an international super-model, famous in the 1960s for her underdeveloped and unhealthy-appearing body with an androgynous appearance.

Our Miss Twiggy ate lots, and lots more, and grew into such a sizable, beautiful and healthy cat that her name was not at all descriptive or appropriate. She had to be renamed. Keeping the "Miss" and abandoning the "Twiggy," her new name was Miss Kitty, from the *Gunsmoke* TV series.

A few years later, we made an appointment with her vet when we noticed signs of discomfort. We were surprised at the "uri-nary infection" diagnosis, which we associated with male cats. Our vet laughingly explained that Miss Kitty, although spayed, possessed two genitalia. Her male organs had not dropped and were partial-ly blocking the urinary tract. Miss Kitty, who had been spayed, would need to be neutered. She used the term hermaphrodite. Another sur-gery, another new name, "Miss-ter Kitty," as if she-he could care.

Miss-ter Kitty was a cat of multiple identities.

Miss-ter was not the usual aloof feline, but a very active, loving and attention-seeking pet. However, when we would take him to the veterinarian, his loving personality changed to that of Mr. Hyde. His people-friendly and purring personality abruptly ceased, and he behaved as if he were a Tasmanian devil. Loud, guttural and threatening noises accompanied his hissing, biting, scratching and incredibly fast and dangerous body contortions. Requiring that he be taken at inoculation time, in a molded crate, as our sole pet, Miss-ter tested both our patience and strength.

In the evenings, he patrolled our spacious bedroom and bath with a strict, no-nonsense schedule, promoting, "Early to bed, early to rise." If we stayed up too late at night, (sometimes television did offer a good movie), it was difficult to ignore the loud upstairs sounds of his displeasure as he would leap to, from and against the furniture and the floors until we came upstairs to bed. Once we obeyed, he assumed a persona of sweetness, jumped into bed with us, purred as he rolled onto his back for his tummy rubs, and fell quietly asleep between us.

Wally explained, "It is not that Miss-ter Kitty was schedule-oriented but sooner-oriented. Remember, he was fed only once a day, when we awakened in the morning. So the sooner we got to bed, the sooner we would awaken and the sooner he would be fed and played with."

And his love was not schedule-oriented either. We were grateful for the countless kisses and cuddles we experienced with him each time we visited his domain.

Our previous upstairs cat, Rasputin, was a wonderful black-and-white tabby who had been found in 1993, roaming the parking lot of Wally's dental office complex. Because the professionals and their staff occupying the adjoining offices in the medical complex were aware of our profound respect of animals, we were visited by a concerned neighbor-psychiatrist. "For more than two months, we have been leaving food for a homeless tabby, who hangs around our office complex. He is very friendly and has been sleeping on a small cushion we placed in our courtyard. Because of possible patient allergies, I cannot keep him in my office. Does your household have a place for him? Or do you know someone who could give him a good home?"

Rasputin was just love and raspy licks.

It took the parking-lot kitty but minutes to adapt to us and our home. He was not the typical cat. A very social animal with a large repertoire of body languages and sounds, he never tired of being petted or scratched on all parts of his beautiful body. For twelve years, Rasputin, our Valentino of the cat world, happily welcomed everyone (our son, our pest man or any repairman) into our bedroom with a rub against their legs and loud purrs. He was quick to learn tricks, if they were rewarded with a salmon ball. His incredible speed and flexible body allowed him to enter, attack and destroy any paper sack we left in the bedroom. That some of these bags still contained our purchases was not important to him. We were devastated by his short illness and death from cancer.

Because we spent so much time (and money) with our pets' veterinarian, our expectations required that they possess exceptional diagnostic, medical and surgical skills. We were very happy with the caring and professional care given by our present veterinarian, Kathryn Sandstede and her receptionist, Carlie Klepak. And in the past, our pets had, on the whole, received excellent care from most of their veterinarians. The most blatant exception was a rescue tabby with a broken tail we found in the middle of a busy thoroughfare. He had no collar, no tags. Not knowing if he had any life-threatening injuries, we picked up this tabby took him to the nearest vet.

"I can find no identifying chip. His tail has definitely been broken, up-high near his hip, and needs to be surgically removed," he explained.

When we asked for an estimate cost for these procedures, the vet became angry. "I noticed your car when your drove into the parking lot. You drive a big Buick. You must have money. So why would you even care about my fee? Don't you want to save this cat's life?"

We were shocked by this veterinarian's response. Our "big Buick" was six years old. Little light penetrated its back windows, which were smeared with fingerprints and dog saliva. Stuffed in the crevices of its back seat was a several-years'-stash of stale and petrified french fries, which our kids had carelessly dropped.

We felt much more comfortable contacting our regular veterinarian to inoculate, neuter and do the necessary surgery on the cat's tail. In no time we found a happy and loving home for this playful tail-free kitty.

Both children always had one or more "found street

Miss Kate cuddles with Oreo Cookie.

cats—Missy, Taffy, Tippy, Topper, Brandy, Bandit and Smoky, Snowflake, Snowball—all of which were great pets and adjusted easily to being spoiled as indoor felines— except Kurt's Panther. Snowflake was a full-grown cat, whose white fur had been doused with gasoline or a similar accelerant. He was severely burned when we discovered him late one evening running in circles on our flat roof. Although his recovery seemed slow, he was an easy patient, even purring as we applied ointments several times daily. Once he recovered from this traumatic incident, his feet seldom touched the ground as our six-year old Miss Kate carried him everywhere, talking to him as if he were her playmate.

Our few rescued cats represented an infinitesimal number of those abandoned or impounded cats who were fortunate enough to be adopted or saved. Recognizing the cruel statistic that only three percent of lost or abandoned cats were reclaimed by their owners, our county introduced a new innovative program, BernCoSpayBlitz for female cats of low-income Bernalillo County families. This was based on a similar and highly successful program managed by the City of Buffalo, NY, in which free spay or neuter procedures for low-income pet owners were offered by the city's animal welfare department.

Buffalo's plan resulted in an almost-zero euthanization rate of cats by dramatically increasing the sterilization numbers beyond the present rate. The wondrous result was that all kitties born found homes. Santa Fe Animal Shelter and Humane Society (SFAS&HS) sponsors Annual Free-Spay Day. In 2013 more than 140 dogs and cats were spayed or neutered. Both of these programs represent a perfect example of proven programs, which have saved thousands of lives of dogs and cats yearly.

Most of our local veterinarians have prohibitive charges for spaying and neutering, approximately $600 for canines age five or older. Although this price included an initial exam and bloodwork, still… $600 for a usually simple, common and frequent procedure?

My search and queries for a reasonably priced spay or neuter in Greater Albuquerque found only one local veterinarian, Gretchen R. Steininger of VetStat Veterinary Services, who offered "50s Fridays," which was the spaying or neutering of any pet two years old or less for fifty dollars on every Friday. Her dedication, compassion and respect for life was admirable and should set an example for other area veterinarians. Albuquerque Animal Humane Association of

New Mexico (AHANM) offered these same procedures, but only to low-income pet owners, for fifty dollars. The health of Albuquerque's pet population is enhanced by those area veterinarians who generously donate their skills to local pet rescue organizations. The organization, Paws and Stripes, assumes the cost of veterinarian bills and training for the dogs of our veterans suffering from post-traumatic stress disorder. It has been proved that their interaction with these pets has improved their overall conditions.

Thus, most young pets or those from low income owners can be inexpensively spayed or neutered. Some veterans are offered financial help for their pets. But what is to become of those Albuquerque pets not fitting those specifications? Can most pet owners pay that hefty fee for spaying and neutering? It appears that it is much less expensive not to rescue a stray animal on your own, but instead, only adopt from a rescue organization. There seems to be no middle ground. Could this be one reason why our city has so many homeless pets?

Could any of these innovative sterilization plans be workable in your community? Could they be modified to include companion animals five years of age or older? Could those income-qualified programs of AHANM or the Limited Veterinary Care clinic of SFAS&HS be useful for low-income, indigent families or senior citizens in your community? Do you care enough to become involved, to research and study these plans and possibly to introduce one to your city government?

Bear's bright eyes always made direct contact with yours.

CHAPTER 21

BEARLY

"To err is human, to forgive, canine."

– Anonymous

On a blustery March morning in 2010, Wally returned from retrieving the morning paper on our driveway. He was carrying something furry in his arms. "Kate, when I reached down to pick up the *Journal,* there he was, showering my cheek with kisses. What do you think?"

"I think he chose a great rest-stop. He is adorable, and probably hungry, too. Does he have any identification?" I asked hopefully.

He was not wearing a collar, so without an examination, we both knew the obvious answer to that foolish question. He was most likely "placed" specifically in our driveway. Most of the dogs we rescued in our neighborhood were intentionally left here by their irresponsible, uncaring owners who, by relinquishing ownership, hoped that someone else would assume the responsibilities for the welfare of their throw-aways. Most animals were untraceable because they had not been chipped. In the calloused minds of these pet owners, their dogs and cats were disposable, like Kleenex tissues.

Our new rescue had not been neutered and needed inoculations, so until his veterinarian appointment, he resided on a soft bed in an igloo home, situated in one of our three outdoor, chain-link kennels. He seemed content, didn't bark and scarfed down our food.

An ad was quickly placed in the *Albuquerque Journal's* "Found Pets." "Red, short-haired, young dog found near Manzano Mts." For safety, I kept the description vague and directed replies to a rented post office box at the *Journal.* Not only was space limited in these free ads, but caution must be taken not to impart too much information so that the pet would not be claimed by a stranger. Newspaper ads had become one of the sources for the bait-animals used by the unsavory individuals who operated dogfights. My "found pet data" also went electronically to lost-and-found pet websites in our Greater Albuquerque area.

We did not expect or receive any calls concerning our "found dog," so he became one of "the guys." His overall appearance was that of a cuddly teddy bear with a comical smile, so we named him Bear. Our vet explained that his tiny drop-envelope ears, long, arched bushy tail, black tongue and wrinkles on the brow and shoulders were indicative of a Chinese Shar-pei and Chow Chow cross.

Both breeds came from mainland China. The Chows were actually on display as the "Wild Dog of China" at the London Zoo until Queen Victoria, a dog fancier, adopted one in the middle 1800s and was credited with saving the breed. Another interesting fact about this breed was that recent genetic discoveries revealed that the Chow Chow had the second-greatest wolf-like DNA of all dog breeds. The Shar-Pei was also among the very few breeds (fewer than ten) with the majority of its DNA being wolf-like. Contrary to what you might think, all this wolf-like DNA in Bear had produced an incredibly sweet dog, who was always eager to be next to you, wherever, whenever, wagging his tail. He never tired of being petted or loved.

At our first visit with our veterinarian, we called attention to the edema in his left leg. Lab tests (comprehensive blood work, X-rays and ultrasound) failed to pinpoint the cause. When it worsened in May, we drove him to the Veterinary Teaching Hospital at Colorado State University in Fort Collins, CO, more than five hundred miles to the north. Although his condition, termed primary lymphedema, was obvious, the Colorado veterinarians were still not able to diagnose the underlying cause. Over the years, the swelling continued to increase slowly, but Bear did not seem bothered by this development. It did not interfere with his endless hours roughhousing with best-bud Rex, a Golden Retriever whom we found a year later.

Bear was not only hampered with poor eyesight and hearing, but he also had a very unusual and quirky personality, which knowledgeable friends of mine attributed to his breeding. Even after attending obedience classes, he was still reluctant to respond to our commands, particularly when he was outdoors. Inside he was hesitant to accept any treat, with the exception of his favorite, pizza crust. But our Bear was never hesitant about loving you. He was the constant kisser, our constant shadow. His attention and affection were ceaseless, totally unlike Clio, who for more than eleven years violently shunned our "kiss-kooties." We soon learned that Bear was a real "ladies' man." When inquiring about our pets, our female friends and relatives always asked about one specific pet, "their charming Bear." And each new day also found Bear becoming a more accommodating member of our family and a more accepted member by "the guys."

"I agree that Bear is still a work in progress," Wally smiled, "but so are we."

Rex was our "Door-able" greeter.

CHAPTER 22

OUR KING OF HEARTS

"I could wish nothing better for animal or human than the relationship we enjoyed with our dogs, Bro and Tracy."

– Joyce Fay, Bro and Tracy Animal Welfare Inc.

The summer of 2011 was a season of abandonment for many canines in my neighborhood. In June, a friend who lived nearby alerted us to a pair of Shih Tzu-Bichon Frise crosses marching up and down Wagontrain Drive, a major street in our village. After about thirty minutes of searching up and down that street and those streets nearby, Wally, Kurt and I finally found these absolutely determined and inseparable pair, who eagerly jumped right into our back seat, tails wagging. They were tired, thirsty and hungry, their little ten-pound bodies shaking as they gorged. It was obviously important to them to always remain together. So after we combed out their matted, long, brown-and-white fur, we settled this now-fluffy pair in the same kennel with soft beds, more food and water. Because their only identification was a city license, we phoned, hoping to return these sweet dogs to their owners, whom we knew had to be distraught over their disappearance. Once the administration at our City Animal Services entered the license information in their data base, they explained that they were permitted only to give us the name of the veterinarian clinic where the dogs were vaccinated.

By this time, it was late on Saturday evening, requiring us to wait until the clinic opened on Monday morning. But after that phone call, we were disappointed that the clinic's information about these two precious dogs was scarce—no name, only a phone number and address. The telltale beeps and recording told us that the owner's phone was not in working order. We made a home visit about a mile to the west, without results. After leaving an informative note on the front door, we spoke with two of their neighbors, one of whom had a different, working phone number for the owners. We called and visited repeatedly for the next ten days, leaving many vocal and written messages. We spoke again and again with their neighbors, *"Were they on vacation?"* They shook their heads and assured us that the family was at home.

Oblivious to our frustration in locating their owners, both dogs showed no stress in their new environment. They were incredibly cute, healthy, happy and well fed, bounding around the house, enjoying each other and trying to make play with "the guys." After continuing this routine for almost two weeks, we thought it best to contact a local small dog rescue so these two could be put up for adoption. We knew that these two well-behaved sweethearts would easily find a new home, if their mute, uncommunicative owners would only release them. So, I taped another note—my last—on the owner's residence door, explaining our proposed action which needed their signature of release.

Jackpot! That did the trick! The owner and her teenage daughter were at our door that evening. "We are a busy family and have better things to do than run around after our dogs," the mother fussed as she angrily snatched both dogs from our arms and departed. No questions about the dogs' care or health. That one gruff sentence was her only communication with us.

Only a few months later in August, we encountered another castaway as we were driving from our home. We were forced to screech to a sudden stop, barely avoiding a sizable unmoving dog, lying in the middle of the street. After a quick, cursory check, we thought the dog had expired, loaded it into the back seat, and returned home to call Animal Services to pick up the carcass. Leaving it there would mean it would just be continually run over by vehicles using this street. And what if it wasn't dead?

When we arrived home, we alerted Kurt. He, too, examined the dog, but was certain it was breathing and placed bowl after bowl of water and dog food in front of this prone, painfully thin animal. Long minutes passed before this shell of an animal laboriously raised his read, gave us a puzzled look, then ravenously consumed this nourishment. After three bowls of water and two of food, he slowly, very slowly, lifted his lean body up onto all wobbly fours. His dull, mangy coat was tangled with dirt and excrement. He had no collar, no tags. We placed one of our larger dog beds next to him. Wally and Kurt kept watch while I headed for the phone. It was hard to tell. *Was this an Irish Setter, a Golden Retriever or a cross?*

We had observed that one of our neighbors often walked her Golden. "Pat, are you aware of other Golden owners in our neighborhood? We just rescued a starved and neglected dog, large-framed with reddish fur, but we are not sure of the breed."

"Your neighbors only a block away, the Tryens, purchased the sister of my Golden from a well-recognized breeder in Belen. Because they are presently very worried about the health of one of their children, any care of the dog has become a burden to them for years."

Wally phoned the home of the neighbor. "Yes, the dog you found in the street is probably ours. If so, his name is Rex. He has always been a problem. We are not pleased with him and because of a family illness, we cannot and will not take the time to care for him." An impatient Mr. Tryen added, "Do not expect me to come get him. I do not care what you do with him. I want to be rid of him."

Not to sound judgmental or to anger his owner, Wally politely asked, "Would you mind legally releasing Rex to us, for ownership? We will take care of his medical needs and try to find him a good home. If you are at home, may I bring the necessary paperwork by for you to sign? We would certainly appreciate it."

Bob, our friend first and our attorney second, provided the correct verbiage for Mr. Tryen to sign. While Wally was getting the release, he inquired about Rex's medical history and was not surprised to learn that Rex had not been neutered, in his four years, had not had any inoculations and had never seen a veterinarian, a visit we scheduled that week. Rex experienced a quick session with our groomer, Laura, at Route 66 Pet Saloon, always gracious about finding time to squeeze in one of our new rescues. The new Rex emerged, obviously a Golden Retriever, clean but emaciated: pitiful. His eyes and his coat were lifeless, and his walk was labored. After a veterinarian's examination, we scheduled dates for his ongoing medical care. It would be several weeks before Rex would be strong enough to be neutered.

Regardless of a family crisis, how could any pet owner totally ignore their moral responsibility without making other arrangements for their pet's care?

That week Pat, owner of Rex's sister, phoned with unexpected good news. "I have a neighbor, Kenneth, who might be interested in adopting Rex." But this adoption was short-lived and in less than a week Rex was returned to us. Kenneth explained, "He was just not the right dog to fit into my structured schedule."

We continued our search for a good home for this remarkable survivor. The following month, at our neighborhood's annual wine and cheese event, I used the club's PA system to fish for interest in our recently rescued Golden. Unexpected enthusiasm in Rex was shown by only one neighbor, one whom I had never met.

Estelle explained that as a past owner of two Goldens, she carried a soft spot in her heart for that breed. "I'm just curious, but what brand of food do you feed him? Is that the same food you have for your other dogs? Was that brand ever on a recall list? How much weight did the veterinarian recommend for Rex to gain?" She was truly concerned about this dog and his well-being. I was impressed.

The next morning this amazing lady, Estelle, restored our belief in the goodness of human nature, which Rex's heartless abandonment had sorely tested. Surprise! On my doorstep was a forty-pound bag of dog food with a darling pet card for Rex. "Although we cannot adopt Rex, this is bagged energy, a cheer-up for Rex to encourage him to get better." It was signed "Love, Estelle."

In all of our years of rescuing and fostering and caring for lost, abandoned or injured pets, no one had ever thought to give us or these pets anything. Even a "thank you" would have been more than enough for us. What kind of wonderful woman had I just met? The bond was there and she was drafted as Rex's Auntie Estelle.

Rex, too, was busily bonding. Bear, same age, same endless energy level became his best bud. They were both still basically puppies and could spend hours being rambunctious and romping together. In record time, Rex was perfectly relaxed with us, and quickly laid his claim to his

*Bear and Rex, best buds, were almost inseparable,
inside and outside.*

comfort zone: on the couch, resting, head on Wally's lap, next to Babes.

Playmate found. New owners discovered—us. Life was good. He ate well, gained lots of weight (from his then fifty-six to present seventy-seven pounds), filled in and became a large, extremely handsome and very distinguished dog. He wore his lustrous, gold and wavy coat well, just as he wore our love well.

Although he did not shed as badly as Babes (is there a dog that could shed more than a Pug?), Goldens have two different kinds of coats, two different kinds of hair, that shed, on schedule, throughout the year. The following June, we were perusing the magnificent treasures on exhibit at our annual New Mexico Arts And Crafts Fair, a juried show of more than 200 state artists. One particular booth drew our

attention. On display were a wide range of beautiful garments and accessories created by an artist who wove them
from pet hair. Recycling! Naively I briefly entertained the
thought that, with at least seven pets at any given time, of
varying colors, textures and lengths of pet hair, we might
become one of her key suppliers. We inquired.

"There are outlets to which you can submit your dog
hair to be woven into yarn. However, my weaving tech-
nique requires specific textures and colors, separated," she
explained. I laughed. In our house, it was like United Way.
Each one contributed at random, whenever, wherever. As
we listened intently, the weaver wove her particular story,
filled with time-tested knitting techniques including the
importance of blending dog hair with mohair or wool to
give elasticity.

She mentioned that buyers of any pet-hair products,
including toys, should be aware of an earlier investigation,
in 2000, conducted by the Humane Society of the United
States, which revealed the slaughter of companion animals
for fur to construct garments and accessories, a multi-
million dollar industry. This was occurring mostly in the
Middle East, Thailand, the Philippines, but predominate-
ly China, where warehouses held hundreds of thousands
of dog and cat pelts. After the fur was harvested from the
slaughtered pets, it would then be shipped in the form of
garments, yarns or adornments to the States. She explained
that the current law required that the exporting country of
the fur be identified, but of course black marketing existed
within our country. After returning home from the arts and
crafts fair, we regarded our guys and their fur in an entirely
different, even-more-protective manner.

Rex had certainly not been protected during his first four years. We had hoped that these years of being neglected, half-starved and left to wander aimlessly throughout the neighborhood would not have left many indelible marks on his behavior. This had, in the past, happened with many of our rescues. We seemed to have "lucked-out," because he was happily adjusted. But unlike our other pets, Rex definitely had a thunderstorm phobia, a stressful reaction for many dogs. Like a fireworks display, thunder and lightning threaten rain in New Mexico's spring and late-summer skies. However, in the entire year of 2012, Albuquerque accumulated a whopping 5.62 inches of precipitation, a statistic that landed us the designation of an "extreme drought area" for the tenth year in a row. Entering the seventh month of 2013, the precipitation for the year totaled .70 of an inch.

During these few "chance-for-rain" months, Rex was definitely, by choice, an inside dog, only leaving to play with Bear or to relieve himself. Then with the speed of lightning, he was back inside, safe from Mother Nature's temper tantrums. His T-Touch Thunder Shirt, which uses gentle and constant pressure, seemed to be somewhat effective in soothing his anxieties during these weather outbursts. But beware! It takes a master's degree in contortion to wrap and Velcro it into place without catching the fur of your already stressed-out dog.

Standing with his paws on our Dutch door, Rex was our special greeter (like Wal-Mart), with a deep, resounding "rooof, rooof" reserved only for his family members returning home or descending the stairs. What a sight! Hence Kurt's nickname for him was Roofus.

Rex and Bear eagerly anticipated our daily walks in

the nearby Manzano Open Spaces, a mountainous area adjacent to our beautiful neighborhood. City-owned-and-maintained land at the base of the Manzano Mountains, its terrain was crisscrossed with hiking and mountain biking trails, steep hills, wildlife. For years it served as a playground for many other neighborhood dogs, who like Rex and Bear, had dragged their owners to these foothills.

While hiking on these mountain trails with our dogs, we met some very interesting and interested dog owners. A Golden owner shared an adorable story with us. After having her dog, Blaze, "therapy-certified," she and Blaze made their first (and last) nursing home visit. Confident that her gentle, well-trained Blaze would be a hit, she was shocked and embarrassed when he tried to retrieve the tennis balls on the seniors' walkers as well as their bedside house slippers. Blaze, she discovered, was better-suited for school visits.

One German Shepherd owner always complimented Rex's flowing, super-abundant and shiny red coat. One morning he stopped Wally and asked, "Seriously, you did name him Silky Sullivan, right?"

"He was rescued and already came with the name Rex."

Undeniably we fell completely, head over heels, for this magnificent animal who was fiercely loyal and devoted. His Highness was a gentle, perceptive, loving and obedient being. Rex was a perfect name, as he was indeed the king of our hearts.

Turner, abused, maimed and injured, was rescued in 2011.

Photo by Joyce Fay

Chapter 23

TOO LITTLE TIME, TOO FEW TURNS

"Every dog deserves to love and be loved and a chance to be a good dog."

– Bro and Tracy Animal Welfare Inc.

On Aug. 2, 2011, I wrote the following e-mail SOS to my friends and acquaintances associated with animal rescue.

"Rescued yesterday, in the middle of Eubank Blvd., NE, a Bull Mastiff cross, injured. He has a great need to find a family who will shower him with love. This ninety-pound dog, who has not been neutered or licensed or chipped or ID-ed, was examined by the vet, then given medication for pain and possible infections for his open wounds on the shin part of his front legs. These were thought to be a result of his being dragged. Although the vet estimated his age at about four years, these have been extremely sad, painful and abusive years, as this sweet-natured dog bears a multitude of scars and old injuries that have left him with a permanent limp on both hind legs, possibly deaf or traumatized, a mangled, crushed and broken tail and ground-down lower canines.

We have named him Turner after the brave couple who rescued this dazed, confused canine from that busy intersection. Turner would be a labor of love for someone who had the time and a very large heart. He could require extensive veterinary care.

I doubt this dog has ever been loved, and it is unbelievable that he has had the will to keep on living, just in case...just in case he finds the one person who WILL love him.

Although his disposition around us is very sweet, I do not know what his reaction is to other pets. I would welcome your help, advice and ??? We have been involved in rescue of dogs and cats in NM for over sixty years and presently have a permanent houseful-plus, so, sadly we cannot think of keeping him ourselves.

Joyce Fay, photographer and founder of nonprofit rescue, Bro and Tracy Animal Welfare, answered our pleas for help, took many photographs of Turner and posted them and this story online, available for anyone who is interested in adopting him or in helping to find him a loving home. Contact information follows."

Joyce and I received some hopeful e-mail replies (most from out-of-state). We kept reading and searching because ideally we wanted Turner's new home to be in the Greater Albuquerque area, where we could make home-visits when necessary. Home-visits are common with most animal rescue agencies and are in place to assure that the new pet and new owners are adjusting well, that adoption requirements (what is best for the dog) are being met, and to establish whether or not help is needed.

Joyce's nonprofit Bro and Tracy Animal Welfare (BTAW) was always my first Albuquerque contact when I was searching for foster care for any dog we had rescued. It is not a shelter, but makes use of its resources and volunteering friends, supporters and fosters to help lost or abandoned, animals (with an emphasis on dogs) to connect with the right people. Bro and Tracy provided an umbrella to other nonprofit rescue organizations in their efforts to care for these animals and supported education that would result in more successful adoptions. Joyce also volunteered her professional photography skills to many rescue and city shelters throughout New Mexico, and for Turner's cause her help was immediate.

On Aug. 4, 2011, an officer from Albuquerque Animal Services Division visited our home and was saddened but not shocked as he examined an abused Turner. He took photos, but explained to us that without a definite address of from where he had come or an eyewitness, no further action could be taken by the city. We were assured that they would check their files for prior animal-abuse complaints in that general area and be on alert for incidents reported in the Eubank-Menaul area. He pointed out that dogfighting continues to be a common illegal occurrence throughout our sizable city, which rambles for over 180 square miles. The officer mentioned one possibility, fairly common among the cult of dogfighters, that both shocked and sickened us. His owner could have tied and dragged Turner behind his vehicle for the enjoyment of watching this abused soul suffer and die.

Turner's life as a bait dog represented the greatest cruelty of the crime of dogfighting. Just as their name implied, these dogs and cats, all sizes, all ages, were used as bait (some for years) to enhance the training of those dogs who savagely attack, rip, tear and maim in the pit. To ensure that the bait dogs themselves cannot inflict any damage, their teeth were filed and their muzzles were taped. To weaken the larger ones, the trainers often stab or electrocute them. They were usually kept in kennels so small that they could not stand, thus had no leg strength. The majority do not live for long. Turner luckily escaped, although still attached was the training chain used to suspend him from the wooden beam above the training ring. Baits are essential components of dogfight training. The prevailing mindset is "The end justifies the means."

Because of their expected short life-span, numerous bait animal replacements are necessary for the training of each dog. When not stolen from neighboring homes or shelters, these blood-sacrifices were easily found at "free to good homes" ads in area newspapers or from dogfight-supplying puppy mills, several of which advertise online.

Dogfighting is an illegal, repulsive, and brutal bloodletting activity. Please, do not give it the respect of calling it a sport! Its gory matches, usually to the death, are staged between two vicious Pit Bull Terriers, usually cross-bred. Not just any dog can be trained to fight and inflict injuries on other animals, because aggression is a behavior not a temperament. Hailing from bloodlines where dogs are bred to maximize aggression, the American Pit Bull Terrier or its cross are the most popular dogs used in dogfighting because of their strength, intelligence and devotion to their master. These dogs can be very affectionate with people but not completely trustworthy with other dogs.

One fight can last several hours. Their extremely powerful jaws leave both animals with crushed bones, massive lacerations, ripped flesh and puncture wounds. But these fighting dogs are trained to give no quarter, to continue their attack, even if signals of submission are exhibited by the other dog, until the death of their opponent. If the badly-wounded, losing dog does not die in the pit due to fighting injuries, the owner, for entertainment and to retain his self-ordained macho image, mutilates and tortures it for the enjoyment of the mentally-deranged, cheering spectators. This dogfighting culture prizes machismo although it requires no act of bravery from its calloused members. The blood-spattered, dying dogs feed their egos.

These illegal matches are held in both urban and rural settings—dingy and dark alleys, barns, basements, warehouses, garages, parks, playgrounds and outdoor pits. In reality, they are just depraved and sadistic carnivals. Frequented by the criminal element, sideshows include racketeering, gambling, drug distribution and the sale of illegal weapons and stolen merchandise. Activities of both could be likened to leeches, as they feed off one another. Often treated as a family outing, this crude violence is presented as a form of entertainment to children of all ages in attendance.

Celebrities, professionals, community leaders and lawmen can also be found among the hundreds of thousands of enthusiastic demented who enjoy these grisly matches in which bits of bone, flesh and bone often land on those spectators seated too close to the ring.

Although their wins in that bloody ring are a source of considerable income for many (owners and betters alike), the fighting dogs are neglected, abused and shown little respect by their owners, whose ignorant creed reflects that the more punishment and pain their dogs endure, the stronger they will be to fight. Their gaping injuries are stapled shut or tended to without veterinary care, as are any infections. Their small kennels are filthy, and their food is sparse. To enhance aggressive behavior, these canines are often beaten, teased and starved. To improve their strength, they are burdened with short, heavy chains, often with weights attached. Their teeth are sharpened so as to inflict maximum damage. Their fur and skin are often sprayed with poison before a match, so as to weaken their canine opponent.

Anyone who suspects that dogfighting is occurring in their neighborhood should contact their city animal services anonymously. And all who had examined Turner agreed that his large and numerous wounds (old and new), untended-to broken bones, filed teeth, embedded nails and lack of immune system were a result of serving as a bait dog for a dogfighting-ring operating somewhere, probably in the neighborhood where he was found. So as Jack Hotelling, a dedicated and enterprising board member of Bro and Tracy Animal Rescue, walked the area where Turner was found, he sought answers, politely questioning shop owners, homeowners and residents walking their dogs. Most mentioned a surge of missing cats and small dogs. "Lost Pet" posters and photos were nailed and taped everywhere: on fences, utility poles, landscaping ornaments and even on windows, gates and doors of the homes. This is often one indication of dogfighting, as training methods involve using these pets as live bait to foster aggression in these fight dogs. The longevity of these innocents is short. They endure slow psychological and physical torture before their certain death. Their suffering, viewed as entertainment, is great and without mercy or mourning.

To help Albuquerque city officials locate the dogfighting site, Jack distributed the photo flyer, seen on the next two pages, for many blocks around the intersection where Turner was rescued.

Photo by Joyce Fay

"**Meet Turner, folks**, a recent case of animal abuse in New Mexico. Turner was found in Albuquerque traffic at Eubank and Menaul on 8/1/2011 at approximately 1:00 p.m. We are seeking information concerning this dog. Did anyone see him dumped in traffic? Did he walk into traffic, abuser with him? Anything at all will help.

In the condition Turner was found, he could not have walked far to get to the location from which he was recovered. **So this may be critical; there could be a dogfighting group, abusing dogs in your neighborhood.** The law in New Mexico has recently been changed, and the abuser would now face felony charges with time in the penitentiary possible. Some justice for Turner would be nice, and a clear message would be sent to the scumbags out there that think this is acceptable treatment for animals.

PHOTO BY JOYCE FAY

And just to be clear, Turner (Bull Mastiff cross) has been veterinarian examined, determined to be about four-years-old, and he has suffered most of his life. Turner is deaf. Turner has many broken and filed teeth. Turner has many old wounds. Both rear legs have been broken and healed without treatment. It appears his left front leg has also been broken. Turner has been starved, and obviously never had any medical treatment. Turner's nails were curled into his pads, and his pads are smooth. This would indicate Turner has been penned up, was never walked, and was only used for beatings or baiting a fighting dog. The veterinarian had to cut Turner's nails into the quick and cauterize them to allow him to walk a bit better. These wounds indicate he was used for a considerable period of time as a bait dog for dogfights."

Jack was disappointed that he received no concrete information from his well-presented notice. Undaunted, he continued to search for information that would help officials locate the underground dogfighting ring in this neighborhood.

Meanwhile, we were slowly introducing Turner to our seven dogs. Turner's demeanor with "the guys" was passive, which was one very large worry laid to rest. Sweet, submissive but badly injured, Turner continued to encounter and overcome new and serious health problems. All of these required numerous emergency visits to his vet in Rio Rancho, twenty-seven miles to the northwest.

It was quite a relief when Bro and Tracy accepted financial responsibility for his many present and future veterinarian and rehabilitative expenses. Because we already had nine pets, and Turner needed an owner who could spend many extra hours giving him daily medical attention and extra love, Wally and I decided that it would be best if we would only foster and care for Turner until Bro and Tracy could find the right person to adopt him: someone with no other pets and lots of time and love.

Turner was the most trusting being we have ever encountered. His many wounds were dressed three to four times daily; he never flinched as we sprayed with antiseptics, poured on the peroxide, and gently applied first the Bactrin, then the gauze pads. The layering continued with elastic, nonstick wraps and tape. He even held out an injured limb to us as we approached for bandaging time.

But keeping this gentle canine from unwrapping those bandages in record time then ripping and reopening healing wounds presented a serious problem. This was in spite of our using an Elizabethan collar, several different types of recommended muzzles, including a metal one, and a variety of thick heavy tapings. Regardless of the apparatus or its content, he ate through his muzzles, including ones purchased online and hawked as "indestructible." Then he attacked his bandages. Veterinarians and their assistants, as well as dog trainers, were shaking their heads because they could not offer any more solutions to keep his injuries protected.

Although I subscribed to "Where there is a will, there is a way," I felt utterly defeated. Both Wally and I were at wits' end and phoned Jack Hotelling for his ideas. His friends and fellow Bro and Tracy board members had boasted that he possessed the talent, imagination and energy to tackle any problem. He invited us to "come on over." To reach his home in Rio Rancho during five o'clock traffic took more than an hour. Turner howled the whole trip, which made the trip seem like two hours. By early evening Wally, Turner and I were sitting in Jack's workroom as he designed a one-of-a-kind collar just for Turner. Constructed of a heavy plastic pail, from which he cut the bottom, and lined with foam rubber, Jack's new but awkward invention achieved its goals. Turner's wounds were not being chewed and reopened, were receiving air and were healing. Jack's talents had not been understated. What a burden was lifted from our lives! Now we could use our energies, instead, to care properly for Turner's wounds.

With violent displeasure, our Mr. BucketHead was battering to relieve his head and neck of this heavy, bulky appliance. These destructive actions forced us to make several more trips, for face-lifting repairs, over the next three months to the always-welcoming home of Jack and Clair Hotelling. Continually obliging and patient to try another, different solution for Turner's most recent problem, Jack was an indispensable resource with an all-purpose, well-equipped workshop.

Turner's wounds required constant care and months to heal. Once his skin looked healthy, we ceremoniously removed, for good, the innovative but ugly bucket that probably saved his life. He would still at times require some method to stop him from chewing at these newly healed areas. What an unexpected surprise when Turner accepted, not destroyed, his recently purchased, special muzzle!

I wonder if this meant he remembered Jack's alternative?

Every part of Turner's condition was improving. He gained thirty pounds, but carried not an ounce of fat. His coat had a healthier sheen. He was sleeping more soundly, and became very fond of our elderly and blind Cocker Spaniel, Clio. She often slept, not *next to*, but *upon* Turner. During his waking hours, he always positioned himself close to one of us. He would whine softly for only a few minutes after we left the house. His warning bark, alerting us to a stranger on our property, was deep, loud and serious. He had become a full-fledged family member, content to be easily spoiled with our treats and love.

Wally was determined that Turner would be rewarded for enduring his early years of abuse. Now that he was physically able to take short neighborhood walks ("turns") with Wally, their bond became even more fierce. To strengthen the muscles in those previously chewed and fractured legs, their "turns" around the block, up and down hills, occurred several times a day, for the remaining winter months. Turner

Daily, Wally and Turner took "turns" around our neighborhood.

PHOTO BY
JOYCE FAY

made new friends throughout our neighborhood. But in May, Turner lost his desire to take these "turns" and began tripping and falling. It was obvious that he would now require a specially designed appliance to support his hindquarters so that he could walk.

We were very grateful when Laurie from Fur and Feather Rescue in Pie Town, N.M., came to Turner's rescue. Her husband, Brad, delivered a rear-support wheelchair designed for large dogs whose hindquarters were not able to function. Complete with padded slings and a variety of bells and whistles, this tube structure on large wheels or tires, was an innovative solution for all dogs who have partially or completely lost the use of their rear legs. Available from a few proven manufactures, these remarkable appliances are size-adjustable.

The April/May 2012 issue of *Bosque Beast*, a publication for animal lovers residing on the west side of Albuquerque, featured the ongoing saga of our Turner in a column, "Happy Tails." The story and photos were by staff columnist Joyce Fay.

"COMPASSION THAT LOOKS BEYOND REASON AND MEANS"

"For thousands of years, humans have bred dogs to benefit us, to protect us, to be our companions, and even to love us. And yet millions of dogs leave this life without ever having been loved or had a person to help and love. Sometimes a dog for whom there seems to be no hope is

snatched back from death's door and given the chance to experience human love before passing on.

One hot day last August, a Bull Mastiff was standing in the middle of a busy Albuquerque intersection, injured and in shock. An elderly couple who knew nothing about dogs saw him and had to stop. As Bull Mastiffs go, Turner is quite small, but still a sizable dog. The kind but inexperienced couple did not realize that even the most gentle dog might bite when injured. Yet their trust was rewarded, and Turner got in their car. Fortunately, they contacted the right people: Kate and Wally, a couple well-known for their compassion for animals, who immediately took Turner into their home.

We know nothing about Turner's previous life except for the stories we can read in the scars that cover his body, from nose to broken tail. The fresh wounds were to the front of his legs, where all the skin was gone. Perhaps someone had purposefully dragged him behind a car? X-rays later revealed many broken bones, never set, and a badly damaged spine. We don't know how old he is—vets guess anywhere from five to eight years. We wondered what kind of dog would emerge when the cloud of pain cleared from his brain. Would he be vicious? Considering the "training" he had endured, he might even have the right to be. In spite of everything, the spirit that emerged wagged his tail and gave love and appreciation. His new protectors had known that all along.

The months went by, and Kate and Wally continued to nurse Turner back to health. Keeping his legs wrapped was practically a full-time job, made more difficult by his special talent for quickly destroying e-collars. Several people were interested in adopting him, but as it became apparent how much ongoing care he would need, Kate and Wally realized he would be theirs for keeps. Nobody can say how long this badly damaged body can go on, but he will be loved and cared for as long as he is here. "Til death do us part," I think I heard it said.

Eventually the bandages came off, and it was about then that Turner swallowed a tennis ball. It seems he does not always behave in his own best interest. Surgery and many vet bills later, he has recovered from that set-back and is regaining some weight. Unfortunately, he still must wear a muzzle when not in sight of his people, as he will chew on his injured legs if he gets the opportunity.

A few days ago, I accompanied Wally, Kate and Turner on the short walk they enjoy every day. Due to his spinal injuries, it is getting harder for him to walk, but nobody is giving up. They are now researching the wheelchairs that have extended the lives of many dogs.

Not many of us are able to give our time and resources as unselfishly as Kate and Wally, but I can see that Turner is doing all he can to repay them with love and kisses and a wagging tail. I know that they feel well rewarded."

Late in May, almost overnight, our strong, sweet Turner developed a very painful ear infection, which two veterinarians agreed, because of its proximity to his brain, was critical. His immune system, compromised by his early years of neglect and abuse in captivity, was his biggest enemy. We prayed that their many prescribed medications would help this life-threatening condition.

But after a week, it was obvious by the swelling, drainage and intense pain that these medications were not effective in stopping Turner's raging infection. The condition seemed to be worsening. Veterinarians could offer no new or different healing procedure or medications, no cure. It was the humane act to end his suffering with euthanasia. We will never forget his bravery and the surprisingly strong, honest trust and love he showed us, in spite of his agonizing life before he was ours.

Though it would make for a fuller, less painful life, love will not conquer all. It is up to us to take up his battle. As Mark Twain said, "It is not the size of the dog in the fight; it's the size of the fight in the dog." We, as interested and concerned individuals, can take up the fight to help those helpless victims of cruel and inhumane dogfighting.

It is an incredibly archaic and uninformed belief that dogfighting is an isolated, colloquial animal-welfare issue. Dogfighting rips at the very moral fiber of American families, desensitizing its youth and serving as a backdrop for violent and dangerous criminal activities. It is not just a crime against animals but a crime against life, leaving a bloody trail of brutally injured, maimed animals who suffer from many forms of neglect and abuse from birth, usually resulting in their deaths.

Many of us involved in animal welfare were sure that the 2007 dogfighting crimes and conviction of NFL quarterback Michael Vick would tighten legislation and heighten awareness of this brutal and blatant form of animal abuse. He served a 548-day sentence, mostly in Leavenworth Federal Prison in Kansas, for the procuring and training of fighting dogs. His conviction was also for promoting gambling and the interstate transporting of the animals. Dogs from six states traveled to Vick's Virginia property, where single-match purses exceeded $20,000. His indictment for mortally abusing fighting dogs detailed Vick's personal grisly beatings, stranglings and electrocutions of his losing dogs. Although upon his 2009 release from prison he was shunned by his former Atlanta Falcons team, Vick signed as the starting quarterback for the Philadelphia Eagles that year.

Those media stories of Vick's inexcusable animal violence were responsible for the formation of an Animal Humane Association of New Mexico (AHANM) outreach program, 505 Pit Crew, which served to educate our youth about the brutality and dangers of dogfighting and, at the same time, offered free dog training. By age nine, many American youth have already been introduced to dogfighting by either their families or by gangs. Dogfighting is an easy means used by gangs to desensitize its younger members to violence. Youths are presented by gang members with a young puppy and asked to raise it. A few years later, most are called upon to enter it in a dogfight. Some are simply asked to kill their loving companion.

These at-risk youths are also easily influenced by today's hip-hop and rap cultures. Often the performers, their music and lyrics actually glorify dogfighting. National headlines reveal that some rap singers even used children's toy and clothing advertisements to promote dogfighting.

The exposé of Vick's crimes was also instrumental in the 2007 creation of New Mexico's Animal-Cruelty Task Force and its toll-free, twenty-four-hour hotline to act upon tips regarding suspected animal fighting and animal cruelty. However, manipulative violators were aware that New

Mexico's laws had a lot of wiggling spaces between their few sharp teeth, making a conviction a difficult judgment to reach.

The Humane Society of the United States (HSUS) offered a $5,000 reward to individuals whose information would lead to the arrest and conviction of anyone involved in dogfighting. Any activity related to dogfighting which was reported would be instrumental in making our communities safer places for all living beings.

Although dogfighting is a felonious offense in all states, the penalties carry a wide variation of fines and punishments, some a mere slap on the wrist. Available online is the interesting and varying information contained in the statutory citations of each state. Not only should you be aware of current legislation, but you might also check online to ascertain how your elected government officials voted on proposed laws regarding this grisly form of animal abuse.

As if in reverence to our recently passed Turner for the endless pain he endured as a bait dog, the U.S. Senate passed in June 2012, the month following his death, unscheduled legislation, in the form of an amendment to the Farm Bill, making it a federal crime to attend a dogfight or cockfight. It also stipulated that bringing a child to an animal fight was a felony offense. The vote was 88-11. The eleven dissenting votes were voiced by ten Republican senators and one Democrat, representing Alabama, Florida, Kentucky, North Carolina, New Mexico, Oklahoma, Tennessee and Utah. However, the legislation did not pass because the vote stalled in the House.

Again in March, 2013 four US senators introduced the Animal Fighting Spectator Prohibition Act, but it was referred to the Senate Agriculture, Nutrition and Forestry Committee, reducing its chance of passage to seven percent. Check to see how your legislators voted. Did they correctly voice your vote or did they vote to pacify the political pressures from the party? Have you e-mailed them your concerns?

Forty-nine states, all but Montana, list penalties for spectators of animal fighting.

Obviously, it is those spectators who, by their very attendance, finance the criminal activities openly occurring and associated with these matches. It is morally reprehensible for crucial votes on animal and child welfare to be cast because of a politician's tie to either the Democrat or Republican Party. Did the eleven "nay" voters actually indicate their approval of watching, amid the criminal element, animals fight to the death, as they tear each other apart, blood and flesh flying through the pits and landing on the spectators of all ages? Were they saying that dog and cockfighting are acceptable forms of entertainment for the family? For our children? What exactly were these eleven senators saying with their vote? Were any of these dissenting senators representing your state?

Other pertinent information available at your fingertips is the disposition of recently tried cases in your state, revealing how difficult it is to obtain convictions. Because these fights are illegal, they are subterranean, frequently moving their locations, which are veiled in secrecy. Tips to proper officials are recorded, but witnesses, usually anonymous, are not willing to testify because of threats or intimidation. Does our legal community need more extensive training on effectively prosecuting those charged with these cruel crimes? The Humane Law Enforcement Department of the American Society for Prevention of Cruelty to Animals (ASPCA) offers professional help to sharpen a prosecutor's knowledge in such cases. A recent New Mexico's legislative session failed to pass a bill, HB459, requiring training for animal-cruelty laws for social workers and law enforcement personnel. The outlined curriculum also included education on the legal and social consequences of animal cruelty. Possibly this educational tool can be successfully introduced and passed in your state's next legislative session.

Although illegal, dogfighting's prosperity can be blamed largely on the chronic apathy of and denial by our legal system. When law officials turn their heads away from dogfighting activities, we are sending the message that we condone its violence as well as the numerous crime-woven activities with which it is associated. Dogfighting's tie to public safety should produce the cooperation of all legal officials (local, county, state and federal) to better enforce existing dogfighting laws while striving to forcibly eliminate this cowardly abuse of animals. And let us not forget the important inclusion of child-protective services, as the effect of dogfighting on our youth is not just deep and ugly, but lasting. One legal suggestion that would be helpful in our state's slow and tedious fight against animal abuse was proposed recently in Senate Memorial Bill 78 to establish a specialty court to handle animal abuse cases. Although such action could also have a positive effect on preventing other types of violent crimes, it did not pass. Would it be fortuitous for your state to pursue such worthwhile legislation?

Regretfully many of our existing animal-cruelty laws do not contain the teeth to convict. Does your community or state have humane laws and ordinances that will stand up in a court of law? Have they assembled a local task force to address and investigate the violence of dogfighting, its effect on animals and children? Does it have specifically trained units to eradicate dogfighting? Through an Internet search of your state's laws and conviction rates, you can determine how much protection they actually afford those tortured dogs, like Turner, who were enslaved to an agonizing life in the dogfighting world. These abused creatures cannot speak of their tortured lives. Is it not our responsibility to do so? In coming forward, your bravery could save other pets from such horrific violence.

My mother constantly reminded me. "Our vision is too narrow for us to understand, but everything happens for the best." It was a thought that I tried to embrace, but it was too difficult to accept. I had too many questions, too many doubts. However, it was the horrific exposure to the abuse of Turner and his resulting death that brought about my desire to write this book, possibly an example of Mother's adage.

How could I make more animal lovers aware of the ongoing abuse and violence against defenseless animals? What could I do to make them interested in donating their time, one's most precious commodity, to join others in putting a halt to this despicable egregious behavior through serious legislation and enforcement? Could this book be a step in that direction?

That is up to you, my readers.

CHAPTER 24

WE CAN MAKE
A DIFFERENCE

"There are those who advocate, and those who do."
– Jon Bon Jovi

The American animal-rights movement has brought
about a surge of interest and industries advocating better
care for and more extensive education about animals. In
today's rapidly changing family structure, these statistics
seem to contradict one another. Each year twenty-three million homes in America welcome a new pet. More American
households have pets than children, and a child growing up
in our country is more likely to have a pet than a dad. So
why are our companion animals still being euthanized at an
alarming rate?

The thirst of knowledge about our four-legged friends
has continued to produce increasing numbers of websites,
conferences, books, newspaper columns, television shows
and university classes. Now offered are accredited educational programs which raised the bar for those in pursuit
of credible information pertaining to professional or volunteer hours spent on animal-welfare programs. The Humane
Society of the United States in 2009 established its
Humane University, one of three degree-granting programs
in animal studies. Both classroom-and Internet-based, its

classes provide current information on a variety of subjects ranging from animal law to better business practices in the rescue community. But as shelter overcrowding worsens and euthanasia figures rise, it is obvious that large numbers of our public are still uneducated about pet responsibilities, including sterilization.

Pet-related spending has soared to more than $51 billion annually according a national pet-owners survey conducted by American Pet Products Association (APPA). National corporations as well as local businesses have jumped on this humane bandwagon. A great number of hotel managements advertise pet-friendly travel. Nutro Company, with the help of energetic volunteers, successfully tackled the upkeep and planning of several neighborhood dog parks. Invisible Fence launched "Project Breathe" to provide fire departments with specially designed lifesaving oxygen masks for their dogs and other canine victims of a fire. New Mexico's past legislative session considered protective vests for police dogs.

Hundreds of movie, TV and sports stars joined promotions of humane pet efforts including Chicago Bulls forward Dennis Rodman, New York Giants star defensive tackle Michael Strahan, martial arts fighter Tito Ortiz and movie star Ali MacGraw. Many candidly exposed pet-abuse issues in informative public service TV announcements for People for Ethical Treatment of Animals (PETA).

In Our Lady of Guadalupe Catholic Church in Mission, Texas, Father Roy Snipes brings some of his dogs (he has thirteen; only five are churchgoers) to Mass and other parish functions. "Pulpit pups," "ministry dogs" or "church dogs" are recent additions to religious services throughout

America, choosing no specific denomination, only churches that are in need of tenderness.

Several prisons across America, including New Mexico Women's Correctional Facility, utilize an innovative double-duty program, Healing Hearts, which uses dogs, who while they are being taught by inmates teach those inmates to heal themselves and others. Healing loneliness and self-destruction with love, these abandoned dogs from nearby animal shelters are trained by the prisoners, and then in return offer their special canine therapeutic benefits to the prisoners. Hundreds of these inmate-trained dogs are then successfully adopted into loving homes. Statistics from this nationwide program reveal it also reduces recidivism among the incarcerated.

Although our flourishing animal-rights movement has served as a shot in the arm for recognizing the psychological value of pets and their ability to improve several social ills, it has also been an ingenious tool to teach responsibility, love, self-respect and respect of all life. Continual attention by the media has brought an increase in both the popularity and pampering (and sometimes excessive pampering) of many companion animals. It has also exposed us to the heartbreaking statistics of animal abuse and excessive euthanization. It has brought us face to face with the realization that there exists no easy solution to the still-existing chronic problems plaguing companion animals, especially in many backward states. Thankfully, because of political pressure brought by voters and animal humane organizations, each new year does result in a greater awareness and safer laws for those tortured animals in most, but not all, states.

I was shocked and greatly saddened on my past visit to

the vast farmlands in North Carolina as my host and hostess drove their SUV, without even slowing down, past several starving Bloodhound-type dogs, foraging for food by the side of the road. "Stop!" I demanded. "Didn't you see those dogs? We need to take them to a veterinarian or a shelter, now!"

"Kate, as a guest in our area, you are not 'in the know' about an unwritten law of the owners of hunting Hounds in our area. When these dogs exhibit behavior that is not acceptable to their owner, their owners abandon them to starve. It is understood and obeyed by other Hound owners and by their neighbors. So that the DNA of this undesirable canine is not passed on to future generations, it must die. And there is another reason for your observations. Some of our Hound owners feel that if their dogs are not fed during winter months, but must forage, only the strong will survive and return. We have witnessed some of these dog owners become violent when either of these 'understandings' are interfered with by a well-meaning outsider."

Applause goes to Oregon legislators for their Omnibus Animal Welfare Bill, granting judges strong new powers in sentencing animal offenders to prison. It elevated penalties for animal crimes committed in presence of a minor or when there are prior convictions for domestic violence.

"Hats off" to New York residents and politicians of Suffolk, Albany and Rockland Counties! Their cooperation yielded animal-abuse registries, requiring convicted animal abusers to provide pertinent information including photographs for the required online registry.

My state, New Mexico, has not been as enlightened as New York, and its euthanasia and shelter statistics reflect its shameful neglect of animal-rights laws. It follows that our child and spousal abuse occurrences are also among the highest in the country, as these forms of abuse—spousal, child and animal—are all interconnected.

This shame on our state's "Land of Enchantment" facade was addressed by students in our Rio Rancho Cyber Academy.

"Hats off" to their eighth-grade social studies class whose House Memorial Bill 46 passed our 2013 legislative session. This will create a domestic animal abuse database listing those convicted of animal abuse. Its purpose was to ameliorate animal abuse in New Mexico.

Our bloody history of animal abuse and failed legislation to protect New Mexico animals is disgraceful. In 2001, Voices Against Violence, a coalition composed of many impressive and politically strong New Mexico organizations, demanded that our in-session legislature vote to end to cockfighting as did eighty-one percent of New Mexicans polled. But our lawmakers simply disregarded those specific wishes of their constituents and voted to retain cockfighting, another bloodletting disgrace.

New Mexico's sad and shameful truth is that it took six more years of continual effort and political pressure by Animal Protection of New Mexico and other animal activist organizations before finally, in March 2007, New Mexico became the forty-ninth state to outlaw cockfighting, citing extreme cruelty to animals. But the penalties cited, a petty misdemeanor for the first offense, were but a slap on the wrist. Because of the lack of teeth in the enforcement of this new law, our officials admit that this brutal bloodletting still continues unabated in many of our sparsely populated

outlying areas, attracting cockfighters from our four surrounding states, which have stronger penalties. Recognizing
its proven link with crimes of violence, drugs and gambling,
legislatures in those four states defined cockfighting not as
a petty misdemeanor, but as a felony.

While our state's animal-welfare efforts fell short, it is
important to recognize Albuquerque's considerable efforts
to commit to new policies, educational plans and ordinances designed to improve animal welfare. In 2006 our City
Council adopted our HEART ordinance, Humane and Ethical Animal Rules and Treatment. Authored by Councilor
Sally Mayer, after thousands of hours of research, interviews and field trips, the ordinance was a long time coming.
Councilor Mayer was our first elected official to assume the
responsibility to create a more humane and animal-orient-
ed city. She became the much-needed guardian angel for
Albuquerque's pets.

Albuquerque's pets were fortunate to have a few elected and appointed officials from 1993-2013, who were
appalled by the startling euthanization figures submitted by
our local shelters. During those years, administrators and
their employees at our animal services department initiat-
ed innovative adoption programs and attempted financially
feasible spay and neuter programs, which currently were
floundering.

Former Mayor Chavez was recognized for bringing a
variety of shelter pets to press conferences, and daily brought
his own cherished dog, Dukes, to his office in City Hall. In
year 2007, he introduced an excellent program to use spaces
vacated by retailers in our local malls as sites, called "Lucky
Paws," where abandoned or owner-surrendered pets would

have excellent exposure for adoptions. It was the first-of-its-kind government-run, public-private partnership animal-adoption center. Plans were considered to make a documentary about this innovative approach to shelter pet adoptions. Also highly successful and visible are his introduction of the "Mobile Lucky Paws," traveling, five days a week, around the city with twenty to thirty adoptable pets from our city's animal welfare shelters.

Headlines in the *Albuquerque Journal* in January 2013, heralded forty-percent-lower euthanasia rates in city shelters for 2012 in comparison to the previous year. While animal activists were still cheering the humane efforts of Albuquerque Animal Services division, Mayor Berry's office also released the proposed 2013 budget, allotting fifty-percent fewer funds to be available for animal-welfare rehabilitation … just when we thought our city officials were listening.

Overwhelming demands on New Mexico's forty-five municipal and county open-admission animal shelters and impound facilities brought about a APNM and ASPCA partnership that will expand much needed services to these shelters through their creation of Animal Shelter Assistance Program. Has your local shelter contacted ASPCA to explore the possibilities of their support?

Without the legislation and budgeted funds that New Mexico requires for more humane treatment of companion animals, it has been the volunteers and the nonprofit rescue organizations in our state that continue to make the real difference in lowering our animal euthanasia stats, in spite of politics and budgets.

Wally and I had been fortunate to receive and depend

upon the help of many of these dedicated animal humane workers and volunteers from our local and state pet-rescue organizations. Their tireless concern, commitment, relentless endeavors and life-saving talents on behalf of the animals made them unforgettable and admirable. We were forever grateful that, with their continuous and unselfish efforts, we have been able to place most of the abandoned pets we rescued.

In this past year, three of the last four homeless pets we found had been abandoned in our own middle-class neighborhood. One April morning I took a call from Trina, a concerned, unhappy and sleep-deprived neighbor. "Two yappy Miniature Schnauzers were just dropped in my yard late last evening and made such a commotion that none of us have slept a wink since."

After two days of coaxing and chasing, leaving many bowls of water and tempting with hot dog bites, Wally, Kurt and I finally had safely secured these two cuties in our yard. Rescuing two dogs at the same time was tricky. If I were able to grab just one, the other would run away. It was necessary to snatch them both simultaneously.

Well behaved and tremendously appealing, but without tags or ID, Reuben and Reba, a breeding pair, were accepted by the delighted and dedicated owners of Fur and Feather Animal Assistance (FFAA) in Pie Town, N.M. Our driving relay was mapped. Wally and I would drive the dogs seventy miles south to Socorro. Debbie in Socorro would drive them twenty-six miles west to Magdelena, where Laurie the FFAA director would pick them up and return to the shelter in Pie Town, a 115-mile round trip for her. After a week, we missed these cuties, wondered how they were doing and placed a call to Laurie.

"I know you were concerned that Reuben and Reba be adopted together, but their tight connection disappeared the minute Reuben found other male dogs to pal-around with. He left sweet little Reba in the dust. Guys!!" My footnote: Reba was the first to be adopted.

FFAA is a sizable shelter situated in rural, western New Mexico, in our largest county, Catron, with a land mass of 6,929 square miles. Regardless of this size, it offers absolutely no animal welfare services and no animal control. Because of an increasing number of stray, lost and abandoned dogs and cats, Laurie and Brad Beauchamp, along with Sharon and Ken Bostick, began Fur and Feather in 2003.

With the help of the donations and hard work of volunteers, they have constructed kennels and indoor facilities to house more than 300 dogs and cats, all of them ready for adoption. Since their incorporation they have spayed or neutered more than a thousand cats and dogs, helping to alleviate somewhat the burden of abandoned pets in this very rural area of New Mexico. Their website is awesome! The service they perform is awesome!

Their involvement, dedication and humane actions present an example of how you, how we, can make a difference, in our towns, in our states, in our United States…for the children, for the animals and for all victims of abuse. If you could take (or make) the time to make that difference, I strongly recommend a reference book with hundreds of tips and community resources to help fight wanton animal cruelty. People for the Ethical Treatment of Animals published *PETA Practical Guide to Animal Rights*, an informative book about "doing."

Pound pups from throughout New Mexico are photographed and posted to promote adoptions.
PHOTOS BY JOYCE FAY

Volunteers representing more than 23,000 non-profit associations, 501 (c)(3) are devoted to animal welfare, protection and services. Admitted yearly to those 3,500 city and county animal shelters currently registered are approximately seven million dogs and cats. About 2.7 million healthy, adoptable cats and dogs (approximately one every eleven seconds) are euthanized in these shelters yearly. There are more than fifty-three million households with a dog and more than forty-six million households with a cat. Only thirty percent of these household pets come from a shelter. Simple math shows an amazing result if each of us saved the life of just a single shelter pet.

My most admired teacher in the Riley's Switch Public School system was Leta Bayless, the high school librarian, who shared with her students an excellent tip on choosing a good read. "The best nonfiction book is not measured by size, content or author. It must leave its reader with more questions about its subject matter than it answered."

I hope the chapters in this book have accomplished that, and have left you with many questions about animal-rights legislation, enforcement and education pertinent to your own locale. I also hope it served to inspire you to actively pursue answers and in doing so, to create your own "pet project," one which will result in a more humane, safer world for our children, for our pets and for the wildlife in our world.

For the love of your pet, for the love of life, stand up and be counted.

We are counting on you to make a difference.

— Kate, Wally and Kurt

Proceeds from the sale of this book will be directed to:

Our Most Treasured Tails salutes every animal humane volunteer or educator, every rescue group and every animal shelter and any fearless legislators who have donated or spent their energies, time and talents to benefit the many homeless and abused pets in America. Thank you for the respect you give to their lives.

Listed in this book are the following animal shelters and humane organizations, all of which strive daily to make easier the lives of those millions of abandoned and lost pets in our communities.

Albuquerque Animal Welfare Department

American Society for the Prevention of Cruelty to Animals

Animal Protection New Mexico

Bernalillo County Animal Welfare

Bro and Tracy Animal Welfare

Dixon Animal Protection Society

Friends of the City Buffalo Animal Shelter

Fur and Feather Animal Assistance

Humane Society of the United States

Kindred Spirits Animal Sanctuary

New Mexico Pug Rescue

People for Ethical Treatment for Animals

People's Anti-Cruelty Association

Santa Fe Animal Shelter and Humane Society

Sundance Ranch Sanctuary

Watermelon Mountain Ranch

Humane publications mentioned in this book include:

Albuquerque Journal

Albuquerque Tribune

Beautiful Joe by Margaret Marshall Saunders

Bosque Beast

KindWords by Animal Humane New Mexico

The Last Will and Testament of an Extremely Distinguished Dog
by Eugene O'Neill

New Skills for Blind Dogs by Landmark Publications

Perspective by Albuquerque Public Schools

Petroglyphs

PETA Practical Guide To Animal Rights
by People for Ethical Treatment of Animals

Ranch Roundup by Watermelon Mountain Ranch

You and Your Pet Are Forever, Curriculum Guide K-6 and 7-12
by Kate Kuligowski

These organizations have dedicated energies, facilities and funds to the healing, care, socializing and adoption of rescued bait dogs.

Alabama Angels Dog Rescue, Newnan, GA

All Breed Rescue, South Burlington, VT

Animal Allies of Texas, Garland, TX

Animal Rescue Corps, Washington, DC

Animal Rescue League of Boston, Boston, MA

Blue Lion Rescue, Yoder, CO

Boxer Love Rescue, Phoenix, AZ

Hand, Paws and Heart, Los Angeles, CA

Humane Society of Kent County, MI

Lucky Dog Rescue, Meridan, MI

Maui Pit Bull Rescue, Haiku, HI

My Lets Adopt, Southbridge, MA

One Life Rescue and Rehabilitation, Oklahoma City, OK

Petopia Animal Rescue, Leominster, MA

Stray Rescue of St. Louis, MO

Tao Rescue, Fort Worth, TX

United Hope for Animals, Pasadena, CA

If enough of us investigate, question and become involved in current animal humane legislation and hold our officials responsible, then Turner's years of suffering would not have been in vain.